by Helen Neufeld Coon For God's Glory

OSKAR AND SARAH
A Congo Love Story

By
Helen Neufeld Coon

ISBN 1-893270-34-3

Library of Congress number 2005908065

This book is based on the lives of real persons.

All spelling of names and places is given as accurately as possible. Names and places of that era are often as varied as the records in which they were found. In this book I have attempted to be consistent throughout.

The African usage is based on the Tshiluba language which was used at Djoko Punda by Oskar and Sarah.

Dedicated to
OSKAR AND SARAH

and the people of
their beloved Congo

Oskar and Sarah corrections:

The following print mishaps occurred:
- Djoko is spelled incorrectly on pp. 15, 20, 42, and 44.
- P. 29, 3rd paragraph (par.)— "Oskar and the African guide" starts a new paragraph.
- P. 42— Quotation marks should be at the end of par. 4, and after "enough" on p. 101, par. 1, and after "born" on p. 109, par. 4.
- Remove "(sic)" from p. 58 quote and the word "superintendent". Also remove "(sic)" from p. 117, par. 3 after "privilege".
- ~~Remove "extra" and "from", p. 91, par. 5.~~
- There are a few extra periods here and there, one is missing below photo 8. It should read "Village of Djoko Punda. Mission station on hill. From author's files."

TABLE OF CONTENTS

TABLE OF CONTENTS (Cont.)

SPECIAL THANKS TO:

- the late Oskar and Sarah Kroeker Andersson for their letters, photos and encouragement while they were still with us;

- the late John and Catherine Wiens Neufeld and the late Esther Neufeld Kressly for their files and boxes of materials concerning the Anderssons;

- my husband and children for their help in finding, sorting and editing the manuscripts.

- Thanks to Rudolph and Elvina Neufeld Martens, M.D. for Congo and medical advice. Also appreciation to James Bertsche for additional Congo corrections and to Elizabeth Martens Claassen for some of the Congo details.

- Thanks to the Africa Inter-Mennonite Mission for their use of Oskar's diary and other materials; the staff at the Bluffton University, Bluffton, Ohio archives who at the time I did my research were: Howard Raid, Evelyn Krehbiel and Howard Krehbiel.

- Thanks to numerous relatives and friends, especially among the Kroeker family, for recollections, the Kroeker family book and other materials; to Muriel Thiessen Stackley for reading the manuscript; to Edith Neufeld Michalovic and Ernest Neufeld for their recollections of our Great Aunt Sarah and Great Uncle Oskar.

SPECIAL THANKS TO (Cont.):

- Thanks to my numerous Swedish connections: Britt Lambrant, Sven Ohm, Dr. David Lagergren, Bruno Andersson, Lennart Bostrom and Rev. and Mrs. Tare Karlsson;

- the Presbyterian Church, U.S.A. for Luebo details from Amy J. Roberts, Bill Bynum and Fred Heuser;

- Cyril Russell of McPherson College, McPherson, Kansas for Sarah's college information;

- those who backed the printing of this book.

Chapter 1: Little Treasure

The following is a true love story based on the lives of Oskar Andersson from Sweden and Sarah Kroeker Andersson from the United States of America.

"We have buried our little treasure in this hot sand, and high palms shadow the little grave."
Diary of Oskar Andersson

Oskar tossed from side to side on the cot under the suspended mosquito netting. His hand would automatically reach for Sarah. But she was not there. She was in another room recovering from the labor of her first childbirth. The result had been unexpected! Even for 1916 in Luebo, Congo, Africa.

Instead of the warm body of Sarah, he could feel the tiny, cold hand of the plump, handsome child on the stretcher beside him. Oskar woke up from a half sleep with some vague, sad memory in the back of his mind. He looked over at the round but perfect baby – their baby – the product of their love. This little boy would never learn to speak their common language, German. He would never speak Sarah's English or his own Swedish. This little boy would never sing the native Tshiluba songs or sit on top of the gate post of Oskar's childhood home in Sweden.

1

At nine that morning the missionaries of the Luebo station and other workers gathered in Oskar and Sarah Andersson's temporary home for a short English funeral service.

The tiny coffin was carried to Sarah's bed. Her eyes scanned the small but plump figure. She gently patted his arms and legs. She gave him a light kiss on his fragile skin and wept.

"He is so handsome," she whispered to Oskar. Oskar wept too.

The helpers had wrapped him in the blanket Sarah had made for a live child. In Sarah's mind she pictured this little one in heaven with the other members of her family who had been called to the Lord in death many years before.

"Will I have other babies?" she questioned softly, mostly to herself. "Yes, I'm strong and will be healthy again. But if I do have any more they'll never take your place."

Oskar reached for her hand. She wept quietly and leaned her head back on the pillow. Dark, damp, wavy hair framed her strong face.

The short service was soon over. The others, including Oskar, left, carrying the small homemade coffin with them.

"Why? Why? I always thought my body was made for having children. I'm taller and larger than most women — and stronger too. Sometimes I've even done men's work," Sarah spoke to herself.

Sarah's mind drifted back to her young adulthood and that awful Galveston, Texas hurricane that changed her whole family's life.

At the time of that hurricane, with its accompanying tornados, Sarah had really performed men's work. But why was she thinking of that now?

The crowd of Africans sang many songs in their own language as the tiny body was buried in the Congo soil. Oskar stood reverently but couldn't hold back the tears. An African friend, Josef, came and comforted him.

Eleven days later Oskar built a low wall around the location of his son's grave. This process helped him cope with the grief.

Fighting the natural urge to blame the doctor who had delivered his stillborn child, Oskar picked up their former friendship and even consented to play an early evening game of croquet with the gentleman. He tried to put the death behind him, but it was no use, at least for now. He couldn't concentrate. "What did we do wrong? Why did God let our baby die?" These questions kept racing through Oskar's mind.

Chapter 2: Sarah's Storm

"Papa came and met me and said,
'Mama has left us to be with the Lord.'
I said, 'Then we can all die too.'"

Sarah Kroeker, *Texas Hurricane of Sept. 8, 1900*

The milk fever Sarah was experiencing made her fretful. She would dream of a small, round face and tiny hands. Then waking, she would sweat and cry, trying in between to be brave and cheerful. All who saw her, including Oskar, felt she was taking it very well. But inside, and when no one was around, she was deeply grieving but still had hope for the future.

In her dreams, and in her feverish thoughts, she remembered other deaths.

First she remembered her baby sister Elisabeth. Sarah was young when this infant had been born and died back in the United States, in York County, Nebraska.

Then there were the brother and sister twins who had followed, born when Sarah was about eight years old. Cornelius had lived only seven days and Justine almost seven years.

This baby of theirs would even join the older brother Sarah had never known. This brother, Johan, or John as some had called him, was about four when Sarah's mama, Katharine, and papa, Bernhard, had traveled to the

United States from South Russia in 1878. While on the ship, S.S. Strassburg, Johan had become sick and died. His burial was at sea before they arrived in New York July 2, 1878.

Sarah's parents, with their daughters Helena and Maria, had settled in Nebraska. Three more children: Katharine, Bernhard and Sarah were born there. Sarah's papa was a minister, evangelist and farmer.

All had to work hard as pioneers. The children, Sarah included, helped pull the plow used to work the land.

Another two children, Anna and Henry, joined the family. Following this were the births and deaths of the next three.

Genoa, Colorado was the family's next home for four years. Then in 1897 the family moved to a newly formed Mennonite settlement near Richmond, Texas. Railroad posters had promised good land and a good life.

No more deaths followed until that storm. And what a storm it was!

Sarah tossed and turned under the mosquito netting that helped to keep the worst pests away. The nets were hung from the ceiling and tucked in under the mattress.

She awoke with a start. In her memory she was running through water, cutting her feet on broken glass, feeling live creatures slithering past. Sarah knew what she was dreaming about. She thought she had been healed of those memories. How long ago was that? About fifteen or sixteen years? She'd been eighteen at the time. She remembered seeing later headlines with the date of the Galveston hurricane blazed across the front: September 8, 1900!

Her thoughts took her back to the sunny day the Kroeker family drove home from their church in the schoolhouse. What a pleasant day it had been. A Sunday school gathering had been held with lots of good food. The Texas wind blew across the landscape. Mama Katharine had turned to the others.

"Look at our place, how beautiful, and then people say that Texas isn't nice. I'll never move from Texas."[1]

Sarah remembered thinking at the time that this was really something for her mother to say. After all, she had lived in South Russia, Nebraska and Colorado before coming to this part of the world.

The new two-story house had come into view with the outbuildings around it. The family had stepped into the house for naps followed by Faspa, that light Sunday supper of zwieback (a double roll) cheese, home canned fruit and coffee.

A week later Sarah's mama had been lovingly put into a grave with three others from their Mennonite settlement buried nearby. They would learn the extent of the losses much later.

That awful Galveston hurricane, with tornadoes in it, had come, water and wind blowing in all directions. It had arrived like a giant pail throwing water everywhere and tearing loose everything in its path. Their new house blew 100 feet from where it had stood. Some parts of their buildings became splinters a quarter of a mile away. Papers later reported at least 6,000 lives lost.

Chapter 3: Oskar's Story

"Mother Joefina, grandmother Lovisa and sister Ida
were all good Christian people of prayer."
Diary of Oskar Andersson

As Oskar walled in the tiny grave at Luebo he remembered where his ancestors were buried in Sweden and where he had been born. His birthplace was on the farm, Vasterlovsta, in the parish of Dalby, in the province of Uppland. The year was 1886. His ancestors had lived in that area of Sweden since the 1600s.

Visions of his childhood home with the dark, wooden outer walls and light trim came into view. Pretty curtains would still grace the windows. He remembered how five rooms were in a row with the middle room used for prayer and gospel meetings.

Prayer, how he needed it now! His family would all pray for the two of them when they finally knew of their present sorrow. His mother Joefina and sister Ida, two years younger than he, would especially pray.

Oskar remembered how he and his brother Axel, three years younger, sat on top of their picket fence posts to pose for a family picture. Ida and Gustaf, who was then a baby, were in the picture too.

Tears streamed down Oskar's cheeks. There would be no family pictures with this little one. And the baby would never see the rocks, flowers and forests of his homeland.

Why hadn't all the prayers saved this baby of theirs? What did God want of them?

He remembered how prayers had helped him back at Orebro Mission School in Sweden where he had attended when he felt the call to missions. He had been so sick, and he couldn't talk. It had been his turn to lead devotions. Oskar asked a friend to take his turn for him.

"We'll pray to God," his friend said.

And that's what they did. Oskar was immediately healed!

Why then and not the healing of this baby? Oskar wondered. But I do thank God for bringing me here to Africa and helping me to find my beloved Sarah.

It was just two years ago that I first came to this beautiful part of Africa on the banks of the broad, dark and deep Kasai River. The African people, the thick forests, the palms and the tall grasses are all part of my life now, as is my Sarah.

Can I keep these African people as my friends? He remembered fierce treatment of the Africans by some other white persons when they took them as slaves or forced them to make slaves of their own people to procure rubber. Missionaries usually treated them better, but not in all cases.

"Lord, help me to get over my grief and stay well to continue working for You here," he prayed aloud.

Oskar recalled how he had felt the call to Africa through the enthusiastic recruitment of Miss Alma Doering who had represented the Congo Inland Mission in Europe together with another woman, Miss Elizabeth Schlansky, of Germany.

Oskar had broken the long standing family tradition of being a farmer and soldier to come to this place. The experiences of the farm, assorted other jobs and finally the Orebro Mission School had helped him prepare for this service. He had also spent some time at the Livingstone College in London where he learned about various tropical diseases such as malaria, parasites, leprosy, sleeping sickness, pneumonia and tuberculosis.

He knew now, as he had known for the past two years, that being a missionary here in the Congo wasn't easy. Brickmaking, building, medical work, evangelism, teaching and studies were all part of the package.

Also included were constant illnesses, especially malaria, and the ever present prospect of death from these various tropical diseases.

He smoothed the mound of dirt on the grave, placed a bouquet of bougainvillaea at its head and returned to Sarah.

Chapter 4: Strong Sarah

"I soon felt that my place was filled. I could

go after my call."

Sarah Kroeker, *Texas Hurricane of Sept 8, 1900*

Sarah was ready to get up and around. The milk fever was no longer bothering her, and the ten days of usual recovery from childbirth were over. She recalled how quickly she had been forced to recover from the injuries she had suffered in that storm so many years ago.

As Sarah had helped her father build a new home from the storm debris she also cared for her injured brothers and sister: Heinrich, Bernhard and Anna. Chores and fixing whatever meals she could invent were also left for her to do. With fresh milk from a surviving cow and relief supplies arriving by train from churches in the north, they somehow managed.

No one else in their own community had been able to help them because each had his or her own injured family members to nurse. And each tried to build a shelter in whatever way they could.

Sarah and her papa even put up the roof rafters and the frame of the new house. Sister Anna, with her back injury, was even trying to help with the lower work.

Sarah remembered how she did this even while cuts and bruises were still healing. And her Papa had been healing also from head and back injuries. But mainly he had to heal from the loss of his wife and seeing his children in such pain.

Together they had done it! And all of them eventually recovered except Mama who had been lovingly buried in that makeshift coffin right after the storm.

Later, when Papa recovered, he would make trips up north to tell folks up there about the Galveston storm. Sometimes he became sick when he told about it.

A bit over a year later on one of those trips north he brought home a new mama, Maria.

Sarah was glad for the new mama and the new brothers, Peter and Martin, who were born later to the new mama. Slowly Sarah realized it was time for her to follow her own course, a call to missionary work, the place unknown to her then.

She had felt this call after reading in the German language papers about missions opening in various parts of the world.

Sarah also knew her sister Katharine Wiens was telling the women and children of the inner-city of Chicago about Jesus and His love. How she remembered what a good storyteller Katy was. With her kind husband, Abraham, they had been the first missionaries sent out from their particular Mennonite group.

Chapter 5: Goodbye

"Already yesterday evening we said farewell to our little grave. We now have to leave a bit of ourselves."

Diary of Oskar Andersson

Oskar and Sarah strolled arm in arm through the lush African greenery. It was early evening. The two had spent the day packing their belongings and writing letters telling the sad news. Their time at Luebo was ending. Visits with other missionaries had renewed their spirits.

Oskar felt that he should hold Sarah up, but he knew she was strong and well. Maybe she was even in better health than he was.

"I'm so glad you're feeling better and able to be with the rest of us at meals. And it's nice to be able to take a walk with you even if it's for such a sad reason." Oskar squeezed her arm as he spoke.

"I'm doing fine," Sarah replied. "You don't need to worry about me. It's you I worry about. Please take care o yourself. Wait here. I'd like to go over to that patch of wild lilies and make a bouquet for the grave."

Oskar sat down on a nearby rock but kept his eye on the area near where Sarah was. In this country you always had to be careful. He began to think back of how it had been for him here in the Congo before he had met his beloved Sarah. Was it already two years since he had arrived at Djoko Punda that Friday, August 14, 1914? And Sarah had come there even earlier, but he hadn't met her until....

While Sarah was picking the flowers she looked over at Oskar. How much she loved him. She was so glad he hadn't died those times he had been so ill with malaria. As sad as it was for her to see her baby's grave, she whispered a prayer of thanks. "Thank you God for Oskar. He is so good to me. I hope we can be together here in the Congo or wherever you want us to be for many years."

Together they stood silently at the grave. They each said their private good-byes, with tears. Then they slowly walked to the Luebo station buildings. Soon they would be going back to Djoko Punda, their own place of work, where they both had learned to love the Africans, the Congo and each other.

"I'll be glad to see our friends at Djoko Punda," Sarah said, taking Oskar's offered arm. "Even though this place has better buildings, more staff and our baby's grave."

"I will too," Oskar replied, helping her over the rough spots.

Chapter 6: Shoes

"Don't get discouraged because I am sick, you don't need to get sick too;
even though I should die, don't let it discourage you,
for people die at home too."

Alvin Stevenson in Weaver and Bertsche

"Titanic dead total 1635"[1] was the news given in the morning edition of the *Wall Street Journal* of Saturday, April 20, 1912.

Papers were filled with the unexpected news of the April 15, Titanic disaster as Sarah packed her own bags to travel by ship to England in the spring of 1912. She would follow the reverse route of that infamous ship. Her farewell was at a Mennonite mission in Chicago on May 18, 1912. At her farewell a special song by John P. Barkman was sung:

"Farewell Song

by

John P. Barkman

Friends and comrades here we gather
Where His power the Lord hath shown
In the fellowship of service
He has made His presence known.
Chorus: Once again before we sever
Let us join His love to tell
And to God commend each other

E're we softly say 'Farewell'.

Lo, the Master has come near us

He has beckoned saying, 'Go'

Thou dear friend hast heard the message

Gently whispered sweet and low."[2]

Sarah's sister, husband and family, plus friends, prayed for her and wished her well. She knelt as they laid hands on her head and commissioned her as a missionary.

Sarah's journey would take her to England to study additional medicine and work with mothers and babies. Earlier she had gone to McPherson College in Kansas for a year of general studies and Bible. Later it was to Chicago to help in the mission work there with her sister and husband and to study nursing.

It was here in Chicago in a little room on 35th Street that she prayed all night for guidance as to where her call should lead her next. The words came to her, "Come over and help us,"[3] and she knew it was to Africa.

When she told her sister Katharine about it the next morning, Katharine said, "We feel the same that you are called for Africa."[4]

After approximately seven months in England, Sarah finally headed for her African destination. Congo was the country of choice under the Congo Inland Mission.

January 24, 1913 was the day of Sarah's arrival in the Congo with fellow Congo Inland missionaries from the United States, Aaron and Ernestine Janzen and Walter Scott Herr.

The four traveled on the Lapsley missionary steamer. The Congo and Kasai Rivers led them to the village of Dioko Punda. Sounds of birds and chattering monkeys were heard on the banks.

When they finally reached the Dioko Punda station, pioneer missionaries Lawrence and Rose Haigh welcomed them eagerly. Sister Haigh was very thin from dysentery. These two had arrived here in August of 1911 and were so glad for the additional missionaries.

The other missionary on the station was Alvin Stevenson, who at the time of Sarah's arrival was gravely ill and in one of the station's two grass huts. His wife and children were at home in the U.S. His wife, Mathilde, had been out earlier under the Christian Missionary Alliance Board.

In addition to the two grass huts the group noticed two other buildings in the process of being built. One was a small dining room and the other a storeroom. The Janzens were to live in the partially finished dining room and Brother Herr in the partly covered storeroom. For meetings they would sit on logs.

A tent was provided for Sarah's first Congo home, and her first task was to care for Brother Stevenson in his illness.

From her tent near Brother Stevenson's grass hut Sarah went back and forth as she attempted to bring down his fever and stop the complications of a cold turned to pneumonia. Fellow missionaries thought he may have also been suffering from food poisoning due to some tainted meat. He had a bell he used to summon Sarah when needed and an African helper.

"Brother Stevenson, I'll get you some toast and milk," Sarah said to him late one afternoon as she was caring for the very sick man. She left the tent to locate some canned milk and make the toast.

"Mama, Mama," the African helper called to Sarah.

Sarah ran back to Brother Stevenson's chair and found him unconscious. He died that same afternoon, three weeks after Sarah's arrival.

The next day the fellow missionaries dressed Brother Stevenson's body in a white suit. Ferns and roses decorated the coffin made from a wheelchair crate. The men from the nearby Compagnie du Kasai rubber company were kind enough to build the coffin.

Four white men, four missionaries and forty Africans were present at the funeral. They buried him in the woods. Sister Haigh spoke in Tshiluba, the language of the nearby Africans, and Brother Janzen in English. Both

Brother Haigh and Brother Herr had gone to Kalamba, the other Congo Inland Mission station at that time.

In the United States the sad task of informing Mrs. Stevenson of her husband's death was given to Mr. D. N. Cloudon of the Congo Inland Mission Board together with Mr. Stevenson's sister. After being told the sad news she took out his last letter, read it and wept.

Meanwhile back at Djoko Punda Sarah was badly in need of shoes. Her only pair was worn out and shoes ordered from Montgomery Ward had been lost or stolen. As a consequence she inherited a pair of shoes from Brother Stevenson after his death. They didn't always fit right, and her feet suffered.

Soon it was decided that Sarah would be transferred to Kalamba, but first she had the opportunity to deliver two babies, one to Sister Janzen, one to Sister Haigh.

There was sadness for all concerned when the Janzen baby died shortly after it was born. Sister Janzen had been very ill prior to the baby's birth with a fever of 104 and a bad headache. Another small grave was made for the Janzen baby next to the Stevenson one. Native flowers were strewn on both.

After these two sad events, the death of Brother Stevenson and the death of the Janzen baby, the station missionaries rejoiced at the arrival of the Haigh baby who survived even though his mother had malaria most of the time during pregnancy.

Following these events it was considered time for Sarah to move to the Kalamba station far to the south along the Kasai River. It was because of this move that she missed the arrival of Oskar Andersson from Sweden to Djoko Punda.

Chapter 7: Twins and Triplets

"So she got help from King and also 3 different
Doctors helped her with money. I took care of
them 3 months and so she took them home."
Letter from Sarah Andersson to Rev.
and Mrs. J.T. Neufeld October 8, 1957

Sarah sat down on the crate turned chair. She was now at the Kalamba station where she had been sent after the two deaths and the other birth. She fanned herself from the heat and to keep away the ever present mosquitos. Satisfied with the day's accomplishments, she was enjoying a much needed respite.

It had been a full day with the usual mission activities. These had included the morning service seated on logs, helping with the school, afternoon language study, which included learning to follow Tshiluba tonal patterns, and her usual nursing responsibilities.

Today she had helped deliver an African child into the world. Usually the African women didn't need much help in this. But this one had been a difficult breach birth.

Sarah used the skills learned in her special classes. She had to be certain the umbilical cord was not squeezed and give pressure and assistance when needed.

Oh the joy of the mother when she saw that it was a man child and healthy. Sarah wondered what would have happened if the child had been a twin or triplets as she remembered helping with in England.

"I would hate to see them take one or two children to the forest to die or throw into a river as food for their gods as is sometimes the custom," she spoke softly to herself. "I will do my best to teach them the value of each child in God's sight," she murmured as she blew away some more mosquitos.

The thought of twins and triplets reminded her of an experience she had encountered while training in London prior to her arrival in the Congo. This case involved triplets. The triplets were born very small and much too early to a poor mother. The mother already had two other children at home and her husband had left her.

It was Sarah's job to watch them day and night. She kept them warm by hot water bottles and placing them near a fireplace. Some folks even thought she should let them die because their mother couldn't afford to care for them. But she didn't!

It took three months until they were ready to be released to the mother's care. Three different doctors and even the king helped the mother financially.

"I wonder how these triplets are now," she mused.

"I must go over and help prepare supper with Sister Janzen. Since she's expecting another baby I don't want her to work too hard to endanger this one. I remember the sad day when she lost the little one back in April."

Sarah, plus Aaron and Ernestine Janzen, were together on this primitive station which now consisted of temporary huts, a chapel and a storehouse.

The Africans in this area had begged the Haighs to start a mission station at this location, and they had complied. Here were the Lulua people and farther to the southeast was the Batshoko tribe. The station itself was located about 155 miles southeast of Djoko Punda. At this station Sister Haigh had taught at first with one old chart and five first readers.

Sarah got up slowly from the crate. Usually she wasn't as tired as this. She hoped she hadn't gotten one of the tropical diseases. She remembered Brother Stevenson's words to her before he had died. "Don't get discouraged because I am sick, you don't need to get sick too; even though I should die don't let it discourage you, for people die at home too."[1]

She also remembered the time when she had been very worn out and discouraged at Dioko Punda. When a break had come in her treatment of the sick she had gone all alone into the woods. "Lord, do you really want me here? Sometimes I feel so helpless and alone. Will I ever have a partner to help me through the rough places?" After struggling, she offered herself anew to God and the Congo work.

As she walked toward the hut where the missionaries would be eating their evening meal, she looked down at her shoes. "I wonder when I'll get some shoes that fit and that are more womanly. I've ordered some more, but they'll take months, maybe even years to come. Well, at least these are holding up. But they really don't fit right and are giving me sores. Yet I know I can't go barefoot. That might even be worse."

Large beautiful butterflies caught her attention, and she forgot about the shoes. And she heard the sounds of birds: the flappet lark high up, the bulbul and the doves. These all helped to lift her spirits.

Chapter 8: Oskar Arrives

"In the evening of Friday, August 14, I arrived at Djoka (Sic) Punda and was warmly welcomed by Mr. and Mrs. Haigh and many blacks whose faces shone like the sun."

Diary of Oskar Andersson

The boat made its way up the Kasai River. Oskar looked around at the shoreline. Tall trees and vines blocked any view. These were different from the pine and birch trees of his Swedish homeland. Bushes and vegetation, as yet unknown to him by name, filled the areas between the trees. Birds flew overhead and occasionally other creatures were spotted along the banks but darted away as the craft neared them. Monkeys chattered; drums were heard. At one point a crocodile was spotted on the bank.

Captain Nyst skillfully maneuvered the boat around the sand bars that made the river hazardous at any season.

"Djoko Punda ahead," Oskar heard someone announce. In the distance he could see a small crowd of people on the bank alerted by the ship's bell.

Oskar turned to his English friend, Frederick Johnstone. "Is this welcome for us or do they come out like this for any boat arrival?"

"This is quite an honor," Mr. Johnstone replied. He too was arriving in the Congo as a European missionary to serve with the Congo Inland Mission. This mission was in a district between the Luebo River and the

Kasai River southwest of the American Presbyterian Congo Mission post at Luebo.

Oskar quickly wrote a short note in the journal he carried with him and promptly put it in one of his satchels. He had promised himself he would keep a diary as he started his missionary term in the Congo.

The note he wrote read, "Friday, August 14, 1914, I arrived at Djoka (Sic) Punda."[1] He hoped to add more later.

Anyone looking at the writer of that note would wonder what such a dapper looking gentleman was doing in the heart of Africa. He appeared more like a Belgian government official or a rubber or diamond mine executive. But missionary?

He was taller than most of the men around him, especially Mr. Johnstone, who was quite short. Oskar wore glasses and had dark hair and a neatly trimmed mustache.

The boat stopped, and the men were taken to shore in dugout canoes. African workers from the Compagnie du Kasai and helpers at the mission welcomed them, their black faces gleaming.

The long dugout canoes, which had brought Oskar and Mr. Johnstone to shore, returned to the boat for the crates, satchels and trunks the two had brought with them. The Africans, dressed in raffia skirts and torn shirts, chanted as they rowed with their long paddles.

Oskar's trunks included medicines and instruments for surgery and a few needed books such as his Swedish Bible, a Greek New Testament, a French language book and some medical texts. Informed that living quarters would be very primitive he had brought a few tools to help build additional buildings. A somewhat surprising addition to his collection of articles was photographic equipment which he felt would be quite useful.

From the shore the porters and the two men climbed the hill to an open place in the forest where they saw a very primitive mission station with a few grass huts and one mud house. Here Lawrence and Rose Haigh gave them a welcome to the Congo Inland Mission.

The place had been chosen because of its excellent location near the Kasai River for the transportation of people and supplies. A spring of water was within walking distance of the station.

The two were shown to a small hut built of sticks and mud with a roof of grass thatch. This hut Oskar and Brother Johnstone would share. It would be their new Congo home along with the mosquitos, ants, snakes, lizards and anything else that might get in such as rats.

Chapter 9: Beginnings and Buildings

"I have received the name 'Melunda Wetu' (Sic) (our friend) from the negroes. I wish truly that I could become their friend."

Diary of Oskar Andersson

In less than a week Oskar was acquainted with the station routine. At 5:30 a.m. came a signal from the station clock. At 6:00 a.m. a church service was held outside on log seats, and breakfast was at 6:45 a.m. During the mornings the missionaries started the African workmen in sawing boards and building primitive buildings which were needed for many uses.

Oskar also spent part. of the mornings with Brother Haigh in the garden near the river. "Do you think these seeds I brought from Sweden will grow in this African soil?" Oskar asked Mr. Haigh one morning.

"We'll have to wait and see; even though the soil is not very good the warm sun and rain should make anything grow."

Since Oskar was the one on the staff with the most recent medical knowledge he was soon given the task of treating patients every afternoon.

The treatment of sores, fevers, burns and knife wounds occurred daily. Knife wounds from quarrels seemed to be the worst. Mud and dried blood were all too often caked in the wounds. Burns were also caked with dirt. The stench was almost unbearable when pus and ulcers had formed.

According to the annual meeting directives, all Africans, with the exception of those employed by the mission, were asked to pay for their treatment at 200 percent above the original cost of the medicine used. Sometimes the payment was in gifts such as chickens, goats, eggs or bananas.

"Brother Andersson, my wife will start your Tshiluba lessons as soon as possible," Brother Haigh mentioned one morning. "Would part of each afternoon be suitable?"

"That would be fine," Oskar replied, with enthusiasm, as he was anxious to begin learning the local language.

Oskar then included Tshiluba lessons in his afternoon schedule together with the medical work. Mrs. Haigh was an able teacher. Both of the Haighs felt strongly that learning the local language was very important. Some persons felt it could be learned in about eight months of diligent study and practice, but Oskar had yet to see if this was so.

Evenings were spent in letter writing to various persons, newspapers and organizations. And Oskar always enjoyed his photography work.

One morning Oskar looked around the small grass hut he shared with Brother Johnstone and remarked, "You and I will need some simple furniture to do our work and hold our belongings." Oskar spoke in a mixture of English and French, and his friend nodded in agreement.

From a large packing case Oskar began to fashion a cabinet of sorts. With other spare boards he started work on a simple table.

As Oskar worked on the cabinet and table Brother Haigh stopped by. "We built our first hut here with one axe, one hammer and a few long knives. And before that we lived in tents. I hope that with your building skills we can begin to build with bricks so the buildings will last longer in this climate."

By Wednesday of Oskar's first week at the station he had also learned how to equip a caravan of porters with baggage to travel from village to village for evangelistic and medical work. These caravans of about twenty porters traveled in the tall grasses farther from the river and also followed paths that had been cut through the thick forest along the Kasai.

Pay for porters had been decided by the missionaries at their annual meeting. It was to be six francs per month with a large cupful of salt per week as rations.

Kalamba was the destination of the first caravan Oskar equipped. This was the station to which Sarah Kroeker had been assigned.

Sawing wood, planting a garden, participating in the services, treating patients and much language study soon filled most of Oskar's time. He tried to include the reading of his Swedish Bible and prayer.

Oskar had barely emptied his crates and trunks from the journey to Congo when a sad rumor began to circulate at the station. Brother Johnstone came with the news one day. "There is told of a war in Europe," Johnstone reported sadly.

"Is Sweden involved?" Oskar asked, concerned about his family and homeland.

"There is no official word as yet, so no one really knows which countries are involved," Johnstone replied as he quietly walked away.

All the missionaries were saddened by the news, both for those persons involved and the effect it might have on any new missionaries planning to come from Europe.

Even with this on everyone's mind the routine of days and nights at the station continued. This routine was broken, however, by official word of the war in Europe.

"Brother Andersson," Brother Haigh called as he came up the path. "We are going to have to dismiss some of our African workers. A message has come from Leopoldville that we will not be able to receive our usual mission money due to the war."

Sadly, they dismissed many of the young African men who were helping with various station tasks such as building and clearing the land. They were also hearing the Christian Gospel.

As pay these workers on the station each received four francs per month and the equivalent of one franc per week for rations. After six months of work at the station their pay would come up to six francs per month. This was a different pay scale than the porters'.

Oskar, even with the added tasks due to the loss of help, was able to continue his time for Bible study and prayer which he felt was very important. Each afternoon, after a cold sponge bath, he would read a chapter in his Greek New Testament, sometimes a chapter in French, followed by the Tshiluba language study. If he was homesick or wanted a touch of home he continued reading in his Swedish Bible. Brother Haigh also called upon him to help with French business letters.

One night Oskar showed the area Africans a slide presentation he had prepared with the help of a magic lantern. In addition to the stories of Jesus, he even showed them pictures of themselves which he had taken. Smiles of delight lit their faces.

"*Tuasakidila Muambi,*" (Thank you) they repeated over and over.

The news of the war couldn't keep the missionaries from their work. Tuesday and Friday morning services on the log seats and Wednesday evening gatherings were continued along with the regular Sunday schedule.

After one particular Sunday, Oskar wrote in his diary, "Although I did not understand many words I felt united with them (the Africans) in spirit." He also added, "My fellowship in the spirit with Mr. and Mrs. Haigh is the best. Thank God for His grace."[1]

The Africans also seemed to be united with Oskar in spirit for they soon gave him the name *Mulunda Wetu* meaning "our friend."

Chapter 10: Wondering

"I am very well in every way, thank God. I feel
definitely that He has led me to the right place."
Diary of Oskar Andersson

Together with these African friends Oskar soon built his first small, wooden African house. At the same time he was looking to the future by planning a brick-making project using local clays. His first achievements were a baking oven and cook stove.

Another task which he enjoyed with his African friends was hunting for game to supplement the diet. One day he took his rifle and his sun helmet, then together with an African guide, made his way on a hunting excursion. As they trekked through the dense forest near the Kasai, Oskar was beginning to recognize some of the trees and other greenery. African mahogany, umbrella trees and a bamboo grove were seen.

From the geography which Oskar had diligently studied before coming to the Congo he knew that this new home of his was just south of the equator, on the same parallel with Brazil and Borneo.

As he walked he wondered almost out loud. Would someone like him from a country on the 70th parallel, in line with Greenland and Alaska, be able to withstand the heat and other discomforts here in this tropical land?

In looking back he was thinking of what had led him to this place. He remembered his mother singing songs about missions. What was she thinking of him now? When Oskar had accepted the fact that God had some special plan for his life, most likely mission   work, he had heard a speaker, Miss Alma Doering, talk zealously about the pioneer mission work being started in this center of Africa, the Belgian Congo.

Alma Doering had told him about a meeting of the American board with a black, American, Presbyterian missionary from Virginia, William Sheppard.

Sheppard had told the board that the territory here along the Kasai river was a great open place for mission work. Oskar had been impressed by the reports of this man who had worked at evangelizing the Africans but had also exposed the atrocities committed against the Africans by the rubber traders.

Mr. Sheppard had even been arrested by the Belgian government and imprisoned. He had finally been released through the efforts of his own United States government. Oskar and the African guide scanned the area but no possible game was in sight. The guide walked ahead. Oskar tried to keep alert as his mind traveled back and forth through the history of this place.

The Haighs had chosen this particular mission site at Djoko Punda because it was near the Kasai River and at a good location for the transportation of goods and people. But they also dreamed that it would have regular mission activities such as medical work, a school and religious services.

This was now becoming a reality. Oskar knew that the Kasai River beyond this station could really not be navigated much due to sandbars and swift currents. He also knew of the other trading outpost and mission station at Luebo which was run by the Presbyterians. He had not as yet been to that station.

Now here he had followed the Haighs, Brother Stevenson, and a few other white persons, besides government officials and rubber traders, into this territory. Would his body, used to the climate of the north, be able to withstand the heat, humidity and diseases here. He knew of malaria and sleeping sickness. What others might there be? Would he be able to fulfill all the various tasks required and learn the local languages? He did know that learning languages had always come easy to him, so this fact would be an advantage.

Another thought entered his mind. If God wanted him to marry, would He supply him with a wife way out here? So far all the missionaries he had met had been single men or married couples.

One thing he did feel was that he was where God wanted him to be at this time in his life.

Enough of this daydreaming, he thought, as he called out to his guide ahead. The guide motioned to him to keep quiet. Oskar stopped in his tracks and wondered what lay ahead. And that was exactly what he wanted to know about his life too.

Chapter 11: Teaching and Trekking

"Today I have taught blacks to write for the first time and to read."

"So for the first time I felt what it is like to

travel in a hammock. It was O.K. as soon as we had

been shaken, but we felt a little bit sea-sick after the trip was over."

Dairy of Oskar Andersson

One day Mr. Haigh asked Oskar, "Are you ready to begin to help in the school?" Cautiously Oskar consented. Soon he began to teach the students to read and write. The station was fortunate in having access to some Tshiluba reading primers from the neighboring Presbyterian mission.

Oskar noted with delight that the seeds he had brought from Sweden were growing fast. Even the pumpkins were enjoying the Congo weather and soil. He wondered what his Swedish friends would think of these Swedish seeds growing in the heart of Africa. He chuckled at the thought.

Now that there were three bachelors at this station the three decided to fix their own meals and run their own household with the help of their houseboys. Each of them had one boy to help with assorted tasks which included the washing of clothes.

Oskar's houseboy was Bukasa. The Haighs and the three bachelors were the entire white missionary staff on the station.

The three bachelors included Walter Scott Herr from the United States,

Frederick Johnstone from England, who had arrived with Oskar, and, of course, Oskar himself. Brother Herr had arrived in 1912 so he was the most experienced of the three concerning local foods and culture.

One day Oskar and Brother Herr were making a schedule for the cooking chores when Oskar asked, "I understand you had a difficult time when you first came to Congo."

"Yes, I was even poisoned by an African," Brother Herr replied pointing to his throat and making a face.

"How did that happen?"

"I had treated a young man for an illness with some medicine. Then the young man died. The relatives blamed me for his death. To make amends I hired the brother to be my cook, but the father slipped some poison into my food. I suffered terribly with sores on my tongue and throat."

"I guess God spared you for some purpose."

"I hope no one else has to go through that," Brother Herr added as the two once again set about planning household schedules. "We'd better check this plan with Brother Johnstone to see if he agrees."

The three had decided to each take one week of meal planning and cooking at a time using the provisions of the garden, the store room and what they had brought with them, if anything.

The three men also used their rifles in hunting for assorted game such as guinea fowl, antelope and monkey. The Africans were a big help in directing them to locations where these could be found.

School classes were changed to the mornings. Oskar continued to take his turn at teaching as did the others. Oskar even inserted gymnastics into the curriculum.

In addition to all these regular duties, there were village evangelism trips to plan and execute. One day Brother Haigh spoke to Oskar, "I would like you to make a village evangelism trip with me. I think you are ready."

"How long will we be gone?" Oskar asked, wondering what he would need to take along.

"It will take about ten to fourteen days depending on many things including weather, the reception by the Africans and other persons and, of course, the ever present risk of illness."

Oskar helped to pack the tents, food supplies, medicines and teaching supplies they would need for the caravan. He wondered how his body would respond to the trip and if he was taking the proper items.

In a few days their preparations were complete. The chanting and songs of the porters was heard as they made their way on the paths through the thick forest. Thorny bushes, swinging vines and leafy foliage brushed against Oskar's face. A cloud of butterflies flew past. He was being carried part of the way on a hammock by four porters holding long poles.

At times Oskar was a bit sea sick from the hammock ride. Brother Haigh, however, was already familiar with this travel mode.

While protecting his eyes as much as possible, Oskar watched the varied scenery. High ledges, deep valleys, majestic trees, swampy places and small streams were seen. Even the temperatures varied. The plateaus were hot and the valleys cool. Fallen trees provided bridges over some streams.

The porters carried the baskets and crates of supplies on their heads, shoulders, or tied on poles between persons. After a fast three hour trek, the caravan stopped at one village where a service was held with a group of Africans who appeared very fierce to Oskar with their elaborately painted faces and spears.

In the early afternoon part of the caravan reached the village of Chief Tshimanga where the group planned to stay for the night. Several hours later their remaining porters arrived. Treating wounds, ulcers and fevers started the evening for the two missionaries. A service with simple language and pictures followed. Stories of Jesus were told and of His love for each of them and how He died for them.

This pattern was repeated the next day with an early start and with stops at various villages where the Africans pressed around them. The Bible message was delivered the best that Brother Haigh could do with his limited use of the local languages plus interpreters if available. Some villages promised to send boys to the mission school.

An even earlier start the next day gave the caravan a chance to arrive at Chief Fwamba's village before the evening. The group planned to stay there over Sunday. Surrounding the village were large cassava (or manioc) gardens, a mainstay of the Africans' diet. Oskar noted the leafy bushes about four or five feet high. He had tasted the leaves as greens and the roots which had been soaked in water, dried and then pounded into a flour, and eaten as a thick paste.

In the center of the village Oskar saw a large bell put there to scare away the rain and a box of African medicine which probably contained teeth, bones, hair, etc.

Oskar neared the box, and the Africans became agitated.

"We will all die if you open it," they explained in words and gestures until Oskar finally understood what they meant. Oskar carefully asked them questions as best he could with his limited language skills and an interpreter. Finally he went in with the Africans to the gods' hut where the Africans tried to explain to him the capabilities of their gods and other beliefs which they held. But their communication was limited.

"These Africans are mostly animists who believe strongly in the spirit world." Brother Haigh explained later. "They believe in conscious life in nature and natural objects. One of their big fears is being snatched away by spirits."

"We really have much work to do here to teach them about the true God and his love for them," Oskar replied as he shooed the mosquitos away from his face.

That evening Brother Haigh and Oskar again followed the usual procedure of treating the sick and wounded that were brought to them. One patient had a large leg wound caused by the stabbing of an angry "friend." The tendon was severed, and the wound reached to the bone. Oskar did the best he could in treating the wound although the wound itself was too old to sew together properly.

Noting a man and woman decorated in stripes of white lime, Oskar asked one of the porters the meaning of this. The porter explained that these were the parents of twins. Oskar eagerly went into the hut to see the two babies. Only one child was visible.

"Where is the other child?" Oskar asked as best he could.

"The god has eaten the other one," the father explained.

Oskar went to his tent with a sad feeling. "Now I know why we are here to tell them about a different kind of God."

Mr. Haigh explained, "They have probably left the twin in the forest or thrown it in the river."

Sunday morning they continued their stay in Fwamba's village. The people listened as attentively as they could through two services. Chickens, dogs, pigs and goats wandered in and out of the group grabbing attention from time to time.

Oskar's food preparation that day wasn't very successful. He and brother Haigh were taking turns cooking. Oskar tried to make a blueberry concoction. It was not edible. He thought to himself, "I'm glad I never made such a mess back when I worked as a baker in Sweden."

On Monday the caravan started circling toward home with stops enroute. Prior to leaving, the Africans at Fwamba's village presented them with friendship gifts and expected and received gifts in return.

"*Bula Matadi, Bula Matadi,*" (rock breaker—a term used for government officials) the children called as the caravan neared villages enroute home.

If this was called no one would show up to greet them. It seems the Africans thought the caravan was from the government to collect taxes. Finally when word reached the villages that these were persons from "the mission," a small group would gather.

At Lukombo's village a very large group gathered. It appeared that these people had never heard the message of the one God and of salvation through Jesus Christ. And they wanted to hear about it!

At one village the chief was delighted with the hammock used by Brother Haigh.

"May I use the hammock?" he implored Brother Haigh in word and gestures.

Brother Haigh let him borrow it for some time.

Village young men put the chief in the hammock and paraded around the village followed by the chief's queen. The queen enjoyed the festivities so much she fell down in exhaustion which appeared to be a heart attack. Oskar treated her, and soon she was fine. The hammock was quickly returned to its rightful owners.

Once again the caravan continued its homeward trek. At one point they trekked through high wet grass in a zig-zag path. Suddenly they came to a river. The porters scanned the area, but no log bridge was found. There was only one way to cross it—wade right through. One porter cautiously led ahead with the rest following. The porters held the supplies on their heads or shoulders. Oskar and Brother Haigh were held aloft in the hammocks. As Oskar swayed back and forth above the water he felt he would have rather braved it on foot. Nevertheless, he did admire the Africans' courage. Those in front treaded carefully testing for holes, snakes and the most feared creature of all—the crocodile.

Camping at various villages, coping with downpours and receiving antagonism and interference from Catholic priests were a few of the experiences enroute home to Djoko Punda.

A number of boys decided to join the caravan to attend the mission school. Their mothers would pack a small sack of food, and their friends would accompany them for a short distance.

"*Nuashala bimpe.*" (Stay well.)

"*Nuaya bimpe.*" (Go well.)

These calls could be heard until the accompanying friends turned around to return to their village. The brave boys then plodded on putting their trust in the missionaries.

Sixteen boys joined the caravan on this trip to attend the mission school. Three, who had second thoughts, disappeared and returned to their villages.

Finally the weary group arrived back at Djoko Punda, wet, tired and almost out of provisions. The gifts along the way had helped. The gifts given in return had lightened the homeward load. Next time Oskar felt he would have a better sense of what would be needed on a trip of this length.

One thing Oskar didn't plan on was to be sick immediately upon his return. Both Oskar and Brother Haigh came down with high fevers. It was Oskar's first case of malaria.

To top it off Oskar was to be the cook for the week in the bachelors' quarters.

Between trying to doctor himself and Brother Haigh, hoping to keep the three bachelors fed and fulfilling his either regular duties, Oskar found the schedule upon return almost more than he could handle. But this was only the beginning.

Chapter 12: Heat Without and Within

"The fever was already over me with heat and high

temperature. It is characteristic in Congo for the

fever to arrive suddenly without being preceded by chills."

Diary of Oskar Andersson

The heat of the tropics wasn't the only heat around upon their return from the trip. A critical spirit seemed to have invaded the mission. This troubled Oskar deeply. Rumors were also circulating that the Bashilele tribe to the west wished to start a war with the government. Their station would be in the path.

Polishing his surgical instruments, treating cases such as beri-beri, working in the school, and enjoying that more and more, kept his mind away from the other disturbing elements.

The *Svenska Tribunen* newspaper's arrival was a welcome diversion with its news of his homeland, even though it arrived long after its published date. It also cleared up his worries about Sweden being involved in the war.

Little by little Oskar began to feel the effects of disease on his body. By October he was quite ill. One day when he took his temperature the thermometer rose to 105!

What should be do? Soon a pile of blankets and hotwater pots was put all around him for the fever treatment—a sweat bath.

Dysentery followed, with severe diarrhea, including mucus and blood. Oskar took a large dose of quinine since he believed that he had a severe case of malaria. The quinine made him almost deaf, at least temporarily. Shirts and sheets were soaked. African friends and fellow missionaries were quite concerned. Each would take a quick look through the door and then leave. Only those assigned to his care stayed with him. At mission prayer meetings fervent prayers were said for his renewed health.

Almost delirious, Oskar motioned to a fellow missionary standing near his bed, "Please, please, do what the Bible instructs. I think it is in James... chapter five... verses 14 and 15."

Understanding what Oskar wanted, the missionary went in search of some oil and a Bible and returned promptly.

"In the Lord's name I anoint you with oil and ask God to heal you according to the Scriptures."

The missionary continued by reading the words from James concerning the anointing with oil. He laid his hands on Oskar and then prayed.

A power came over Oskar. He began to praise God, both in Swedish and in a strange language which he had never studied. Oskar had not had a similar experience for a long time. However this "speaking in tongues" was not new to him. That night Oskar rested. He was able to sit up the next day although he was still weak and thin. By the day after that his stomach would allow some food. Even after a week the fever didn't abate completely. Oskar, however, was restored in spirit. And he was very tired of the old canned milk that had been his diet for the duration of the illness.

As Oskar sat in his hut he heard the sounds of the Africans singing in the chapel next door. The chapel was now a shed under a grass roof. He so wanted to be completely well to be able to join them. "And why haven't I received any letters from my homeland?" he would mutter to no one in particular. "It takes so long to get mail here." Now it was the end of October, and the only news he had read from home was the newspaper, many weeks old.

"I must fight this," he would say to himself, and he would pray for his friends both in Africa and Sweden. One attraction which kept him amused was the play of the monkeys climbing and chattering in the trees.

On November 7, the homesickness he had been feeling was helped by the first letter from home since his August 14th arrival in the Congo. A letter also arrived from his Swedish editor friend, Bystrom, telling Oskar that due to the war in Europe he would not be able to send the missionaries their expected money at this time.

"Will you go to the service today?" Oskar's houseboy, Bukasa, asked one Sunday when it appeared that Oskar was getting stronger. Using a mixture of gestures and language Oskar was beginning to understand his helper.

"I think I will try to go this morning, and then maybe for the evening prayer meeting." Oskar wasn't certain the houseboy understood, but the boy smiled and helped him gather the clothes he needed.

Oskar made it through the morning service and was heading back to his house to rest when Brother Haigh approached him.

"Brother Andersson, I have to make a trip to Luebo on mission business tomorrow. I would like you to come along to see the Presbyterian mission doctor, Dr. L. J. Coppedge. Your condition has improved, but we're still worried about you."

"I appreciate your concern, but I don't know how my body will take to the trip."

"We'll see that the porters carry you as much of the way as possible," Brother Haigh replied.

Chapter 13: Learning at Luebo

"Around 11 a.m. we reached Luebo. We were warmly met.
The station is large, also high and beautifully situated."
Diary of Oskar Andersson

On Monday Oskar slowly prepared for the trip with the help of Bukasa. By afternoon, he, Brother Haigh and porters for the trip were on their way.

By evening of the first day Oskar was ready to rest for the night even though he was unable to sleep very well in the tent.

Tuesday they reached Kasangishu, a large, finely situated village. Brother Haigh also had a fever that evening. The night itself was much worse than Monday. A thunderstorm arrived, tearing at the tent supports. Rats, dogs and sheep tried to join them to escape the storm. In the early morning the caravan continued with Oskar being glad to be on the move from the night's unwelcome adventures.

Finally on Wednesday at about 11 a.m. the caravan reached the American Presbyterian Congo Mission at Luebo. What a welcome sight it was to the tired and sick group! Staying in a brick house and eating meals at a common table were feasts for Oskar's senses. It seemed to be the needed refreshment for Oskar's spirit and body.

After a personal visit with Dr. Llewellyn Coppege, to look over his own case, Oskar was well enough to accompany the doctor around the station.

In the days following, Oskar could hardly believe his eyes and ears.

Three services were held on the station each day. About 1000 persons filled the area at each time. Oskar also observed the school classes where several hundred students were taught. Here Brother Haigh and Oskar gained ideas for their own station's school. Especially enjoyable to Oskar was a visit to a class in the evangelists' school.

Even the Luebo brick yard and mission farm were carefully observed for future plans at Dioko Punda.

On Saturday, Luebo's Dr. William Morrison led Oskar and Brother Haigh on a tour of the area surrounding the station. Their main interest was a large market visited by several thousand Africans. As they walked slowly around, Dr. Morrison reported some historical details.

"There once was a large slave market here," he explained. "One time when the mother of a powerful chief died 300 slaves were killed."

He continued, "Just recently the government arrested a chief for permitting four wives to be buried alive with their dead husband.

Sunday was a bright contrast to the reports of the previous day. Approximately 1200 gathered together for the morning worship, and almost 1500 participated in the afternoon Sunday school.

Oskar felt renewed by these evidences of God at work, and he even felt strong enough to attend an evening meeting for all the missionaries.

Finally it was time for a return trip to Djoko Punda. This time the caravan took an indirect route to stop at a village where an evangelist had been requested. As they traveled Oskar found it hard to believe that it was November. Here the hot sun and the rains made everyone and everything sweat.

Their journey led the caravan through one swamp which was the home of many lizards and snakes. Oskar marveled at how the Africans with their bare feet were seldom bitten.

Most of the time the caravan porters were very helpful. Early one morning, however, some of the group refused to move. They had indulged in Palm wine. Brother Haigh felt it necessary to take out a whip as a warning.

Both Oskar and Brother Haigh were relieved when its use was not needed.

As they traveled, the Africans took advantage of each stream for a refreshing bath, splashing happily and noisily.

Chanting and singing as they marched the group finally reached the village where their first evangelist, Makasudi, would be situated. These arrangements took some time, but since this was Djoko Punda's first evangelist, Brother Haigh felt the time spent was necessary.

Finally the caravan was able to start on the last leg of its journey toward home. Cool breezes now accompanied the group.

Most of the provisions were finished so the group all ate the native cassava porridge for their sustenance. Oskar didn't mind this, but he would be glad to return to his home and friends at Djoko Punda.

Chapter 14: Ants and Anticipation

"Take care of the kitchen again this week, help in the school
twice a day, also have my language lessons as usual.
We are also preparing a place for brick making."
Diary of Oskar Andersson

Home looked very good to Oskar when the caravan arrived at Dioko Punda on Saturday. After distributing pay and salt rations to the porters Oskar was ready for a rest. By Sunday, however, Brother Haigh was in bed with a high fever. Sister Haigh took care of her husband so that left the three bachelors in charge of the regular Sunday services.

By the last of November both Brother and Sister Haigh were ill with the weaknesses and fever. Oskar and the other two missionaries, Herr and Johnstone, carried on as best they could. Each of them also took turns having fevers and other ailments.

December 1 dawned and to Oskar it was a special day. In Sweden it was Oskar's Day. Cups of coffee and flowers were given to the honored person on their day. Fond memories filled Oskar's mind as he recalled that last year he had been at the region of Hudiksvall in his homeland.

On this special day here in Africa, instead of coffee and flowers received, his activities included draining six to eight quarts of water from the swollen abdomen of a twelve-to-fourteen year old boy.

"You are brave," Oskar told the boy, as the young one patiently endured the operation, lying still and calm.

"I think you are braver than I am," Oskar said softly to himself.

December settled into a routine with kitchen duties, medical work, helping in the school twice a day, language lessons and preparing the brick making location.

One day Oskar and Brother Haigh went out searching for a good path through the forest to the brick-making area. Some ants had other ideas! The ants attacked the two intruders with a vengeance! Hurriedly the two escaped to the place where a number of Africans were working. The Africans beat at the ants with all the skill of years of similar experience. Once again Oskar admired the skill and knowledge of his new friends. He also wondered what other surprises this country had in store for him.

Sweat poured down Oskar's body and insects took over as Oskar worked in the tropical heat to set up the brick press and kiln. Another day he labored to begin a shelter over the brick-making place.

School was not in session for the present to give a month off for the Christmas holidays. Oskar secretly hoped that here maybe the station people would celebrate Christmas a little like the Swedish people celebrated this special season.

One thing Oskar soon found out was that there would be no vacation for the mission station staff. Oskar and the others continued with language studies, working with the two evangelists who were now out in the villages plus regular daily tasks.

Finally Oskar was given the chance to give his first message in the Tshiluba language. It seemed somewhat humorous to him, however, since the chosen location of this special event was a Bashilele village where the Africans spoke Tshitshilele rather than Tshiluba. A few did understand his halting words.

Nevertheless Oskar gave the message a second time at the Tuesday morning service at their own station's grass church. And it was understood!

His illness, village trip, and trek to Luebo had put Oskar about two months behind in his language lessons. Giving the talk had made him feel that some progress had been made.

But the calendar wasn't behind. Christmas was approaching! Oskar eagerly looked forward to Christmas and also to the time when they would actually be able to build with the bricks.

Chapter 15: A Congo Christmas

"Yes, it has been Christmas, but it has not been Swedish."
Diary of Oskar Andersson

"*Muambi*, someone steal our chickens!" Bukasa rushed in exclaiming one December morning.

Missionaries and Africans checked the area but no one could figure out who was the thief.

A day or so later another African boy came running and explaining, "We catch the thief—big snake. We chop off its head."

That day the school boys had a feast with the meat. Brother Haigh saved the skin.

Snakes and Christmas seemed an unlikely combination to Oskar. But that's the way it was in this his new home.

Christmas Eve day finally arrived. Work was accomplished as usual in the morning with Oskar setting up the brick oven for baking bread and other items. In the afternoon he finished the doors for his housemate Johnstone's room. This was to be a surprise for Johnstone upon his return from a trip to Luebo. Brother Johnstone was there fixing missionaries' teeth.

Brother Herr was the cook for this week, so Oskar wondered what he would plan for Christmas eve supper. Remembering the wonderful Christmas eve meals of his Swedish homeland made him somewhat homesick.

Christmas Eve supper arrived. Oskar and Brother Herr sat at the table. The houseboy brought in the food. Oskar and Brother Herr looked at the table and then at each other. What was this? A bowl of fish bones from the noon meal was the only item on the table. Brother Herr jumped up and came to the rescue since it was his week to cook.

"I will go get that extra apple pie I baked on Monday and reheat in the oven. Maybe then this will seem more like Christmas Eve."

After rebaking the pie, it was still a bit tough since this day was now Thursday.

Oskar said to himself, "Next year I'll introduce some Swedish Christmas Eve customs to make the eve a bit more Christmaslike, at least to me."

To ease the loneliness of the evening Oskar spent the early part of it in prayer and meditation. He began to read the Christmas story from his Swedish Bible when urgent sounding footsteps broke the stillness.

"Quick, Oskar, come help us," Brother Haigh was urgently pleading. "Our son is having convulsions."

When Oskar arrived at the Haighs' dwelling the young boy was still having convulsions, cramps and a very high fever.

It appeared to Oskar that the young son, Lawrence, had several teeth coming in plus malaria with its accompanying fever. Oskar had to make some quick medical decisions. Everyone in the room prayed as Oskar decided which medicines to give to the child. He gave him two different ones, and that seemed to have a soothing effect on Lawrence. Shortly thereafter the boy became quiet and fell asleep.

Oskar's first Christmas day on African soil arrived. Torrents of rain cancelled the morning church service. The next item of the day was for Oskar to operate again on the swollen abdomen of the African boy. He had already once drained this boy's abdomen. This time Oskar removed about seven or eight quarts of liquid.

The day was brightened by a noon Christmas meal together at the Haighs. Oskar realized through this that some Americans have their big Christmas meal at noon on Christmas Day rather than on Christmas Eve as he was used to in Sweden. All the missionaries of the station were there except Brother Johnstone who was still at Luebo.

All who were gathered there, especially the parents, were pleased to see that the Haighs' son seemed to be better. The missionaries spent time praising and thanking the Lord for this and other blessings.

By afternoon the rain had stopped enough to continue with the day's activities which included an afternoon of races and competitions with small prizes. The Africans happily participated.

Later that afternoon everyone gathered for a worship service which made Oskar feel that it was finally Christmas.

Suddenly someone shouted, "Lua, lua, (come, come)."

Everyone ran to see what the excitement was all about. In the distance they saw a caravan of 25 or more bearers. When the caravan came closer the gathered group realized the tired workers were from the sister station, Kalamba. These Christian friends would be able to have a bit of Christmas here with them.

When Oskar returned to his little home, he wrote in his diary, "Yes, it has been Christmas, but it has not been Swedish. Thanks be to God for his mercy, peace and strength. Also that I can be here in Jesus' name."[1]

Chapter 16: A New Year

"Today is New Year's day. Praise be to God for the year which is passed. It has been more eventful than any before, but I have also neither ever before experienced God's faithfulness as I did this year."
Diary of Oskar Andersson

The mosquitos buzzed around his head. Trickles of sweat poured down his body. Oskar ended 1914 and began 1915 by completing the brick kiln and starting the brick firing. This meant that Oskar lived part of the time alone in a tent near the banks of the Kasai River to keep an eye on the kiln.

When his African helpers were around he would tell them Bible stories and share the message of Christ with them as he knew it and had experienced it in his own life. Of course the language barriers made this difficult, and he had to keep it very simple. At night he would enjoy the wonder of the starlit night. But at times he was lonesome.

"I wonder what 1915 will bring to me," Oskar wondered to himself.

Medical duties continued interspersed with the brick making. Business duties and language study also took time. He felt he was making progress in the local language.

Finally the first brick kiln was ready to take apart. Oskar was very anxious to see the bricks inside. Oskar slowly examined the bricks. He was very disappointed! None of the red brick was usable. He had miscalculated. As he investigated further, however, several hundred bricks of one type of white clay were usable.

Oskar and the others decided that the kiln had to be moved to the location of this white clay. They would then start over again.

Oskar held a compass in one hand and a handkerchief to fan away the bugs in the other. He, together with Brother Herr and the African workers, made their way to the white clay area. Finally the group arrived at the correct place. Construction soon started at the new location.

By the end of January the brick making was again in full swing. Station meetings were also held which resulted in changes and new assignments. Oskar was named secretary and legal representative of the Djoko Punda mission station.

To Oskar's disappointment Brother Johnstone, who had returned from fixing teeth at Luebo, was to be transferred to Kalamba. Oskar had appreciated the company of this English friend who had arrived at the station with him.

By the beginning of February a letter was received telling of the expected arrival of three more mission workers for the Congo Inland Mission stations. These missionaries were now on African soil. To Oskar's joy two were from Sweden: a Miss Elsa Lundberg and Mr. Henning Karlsson. The third was Miss Anna Meester, a nurse from Holland.

The end of February arrived and Oskar was still waiting for the new arrivals. One Friday, late in the evening, he was suddenly roused by the sound of a steamer whistle. He rushed down to the river, hoping to welcome the new missionaries. But they were not on board. It was a very disappointed Oskar who returned to his little home.

On March 12 a welcome letter arrived from Luebo. The new missionaries had made it that far!

Chapter 17: New Arrivals and a New Congregation

"In the morning we went down to the Kasai River beach, where we held our church service, during which two of our hopeful youth followed Jesus in baptism. (The names of the boys are Kalala and Luaba.)"
Diary of Oskar Andersson

Oskar quickly organized a caravan to head for Luebo to bring the new missionaries back to Djoko Punda. The usual heat and rain storms delayed the trip. Finally Oskar arrived at Luebo. He joyously greeted the new missionaries. How great it was to speak to someone in one's own language!

Oskar also appreciated renewing the friendships he had previously made at Luebo.

On the Sunday after Oskar's arrival there, Elsa Lundberg, one of the new missionaries, spoke to the whole Luebo Sunday school. Dr. Morrisson interpreted. The staff at Luebo were so delighted with her they wanted to keep her there at that station. But she was scheduled to be part of the Djoko Punda mission station, and she wasn't persuaded to stay at Luebo.

Monday arrived and Oskar was able to rearrange a government boat's schedule so that the commander was willing to make a trip change and head for Djoko Punda. That way the newcomers would avoid the difficult overland trip in the heat.

Approximately seventy trunks of personal belongings, supplies, equipment and food were loaded on the boat. The evening before departure all the missionaries at Luebo enjoyed a party! Everything was as Swedish as possible. A Norwegian missionary, Dr. Thomas Stixrud, had suggested this event. The guests from other countries were also delighted with this change in routine. Included among the party treats were St. Lucia buns, suggested by one of the Swedish guests, even though these are usually saved for serving on December 13.

Luebo friends waved goodbye to the group at the river's bank. By dark that evening the group arrived at Djoko Punda. The Haighs greeted Oskar and the new missionaries. Early the next morning Oskar went back to the river to arrange for the removal of the numerous trunks from the boat. That evening, to Oskar's delight, Sister Lundberg showed photos from Sweden to the gathered missionaries.

Sunday arrived. Oskar woke up with unusual anticipation. First, it was his 29th birthday. Second, he looked forward to continued fellowship and worship with the new arrivals. His joy was shortlived however.

Brother Haigh approached Oskar and stated, "Oskar, I want you to go today to an outside village for meetings."

Oskar pleaded in response, "Today is my birthday and the first Sunday my friends from Sweden are here. Couldn't I go another Sunday?"

Brother Haigh was not pleased with Oskar's answer. He himself went to the outside village.

On Monday Oskar approached Brother Haigh, "I believe you made a mistake yesterday and should have stayed home to welcome the new arrivals."

"No, we are here to reach these Africans for Christ, not to have time off whenever we choose!"

With that they each went their own way and Oskar didn't feel like speaking to Brother Haigh the rest of that day. Brother Haigh seemed to feel the same way.

On Tuesday the two met together and resolved their dispute. They were friends again! The strained relationship of one Sunday was turned to true joy when the next Sunday two young African believers, Kalala and Luaba, were baptized in the Kasai River!

Two other Africans who had received their baptism certificates from Luebo and the two new converts were the official start of the Djoko Punda congregation!

Chapter 18: Cleaning and Communion

*"Surprisingly I have cleaned my house so that it looks
very nice in my grass castle."*
Diary of Oskar Andersson

By the end of March Oskar was being trained by Brother Haigh to handle the mission's business. The Haighs would be leaving shortly for a furlough to the United States. Oskar would be in charge of the Djoko Punda station.

In the ensuing staff changes Sister Meester would be going to Kalamba, and a caravan, led by Brother Herr, would soon be arriving from there. Oskar had heard that a missionary from Kalamba, one Miss Sarah Kroeker, would be coming to work here at Djoko Punda. He knew that she was a Mennonite from the United States and a trained nurse. Reports were that she was very caring and friendly. Those who had worked with her had great respect for her. She seemed to have a special love for babies.

Meanwhile at Djoko Punda, Sister Lundberg took over some of the school work which gave Oskar extra time for working at the brickyard. In the afternoons he taught Tshiluba to Brother Karlsson. In between he continued his own language studies.

One unusually bright day Oskar looked at his small African hut and decided it was time to give it a thorough cleaning. Diligently he scrubbed, removed debris, dusted the few items he owned and put things all in an orderly fashion. He was very proud of himself, a bachelor, putting it in such good shape.

"It does look rather lonely, though," he muttered. "Maybe it needs a few flowers or something that a woman might add to make it truly homey." Oskar could really tell that he was homesick for his family and the Swedish touches such as flowers, good coffee and friends coming to call. Wildflowers were added.

Africans came running to call on an evening a few days later. "Crocodile dead at brickyard!" Oskar's houseboy called to Oskar from a long way off. Oskar checked the story and there truly had been a crocodile killed at his own place of work.

The brickyard also had other surprises. The second set of bricks turned out to be in excellent condition. Oskar was greatly pleased. This would mean that the new house that had been in the planning for some time could be built. And it would last much longer than the present huts. The house was soon planned and the dimensions were laid on the ground. In addition a less steep road to the brick yard was built to aid in bringing the bricks to the place of construction. Brothers Karlsson and Herr would be of great help in the building of the house.

Crocodiles, bricks, building and cleaning did not keep the missionaries from their most important task of bringing the good news of Jesus Christ to the people of the area.

As a result of the recent baptisms and official organization of the Djoko Punda congregation, a communion service was held for the first time with the newly formed group. This memorable Sunday was April 4, 1915. Oskar was so disappointed that his stomach was bothering him, and he was unable to attend.

"Will I ever get over these illnesses?" he said dejectedly. "At least I can stay here and pray and read my Swedish Bible, but I'm not even sure I feel good enough to do that."

By afternoon, however, he was feeling somewhat better so he took part in the Sunday school and evening meetings. His stomach was still not up to eating or drinking much except tea.

Oskar tried his best to keep the mosquitos away. Even the netting around the cot couldn't keep them all out. And the heat was once again around him. Here he was again in a tent, in the jungle, near the beach both night and day. It was his job to watch the new brick kiln that had just recently been fired.

By the end of April all of Djoko Punda was excited by the news that the long awaited caravan from Kalamba would soon be arriving! Word was delivered to Oskar at the brickyard.

Chapter 19: Reflection and Responsibility

"Motion made by Bro. Claudon, that Sister Kroeker act as superintendent, (sic)sec'y and official representative on the field, during the absence of Bro. and Sister Haigh, assisted by Bro. Andersen (sic) when she so requests. Sec'nd & Carried"
Records of the Congo Indland Mission Board
Spelling as in the minutes of Dec. 22, 1914

Sarah tied the large, recently polished, leather shoes tightly. These men's shoes were still her only shoes, and as yet they didn't fit. She was developing sores on her feet.

Sarah and the porters had been awakened early to start the last leg of the trek to Djoko Punda.

"How I wish my shoes hadn't been lost from that Montgomery Ward order, or stolen. Or I wish others had arrived. Then I would have decent shoes for my work here. And my only other pair was completely worn."

She slipped into the long cotton dress with its tiny print that she had brought with her from the United States. It still fit. She had kept it washed, starched and mended all this time so it would have longer wear.

With the onset of the war even material for dresses was scarce. She had to carefully maintain the few items she had. Fortunately she had one or two nurses' uniforms she could wear for her work.

"I'd like to look my best when I arrive at my new assignment, despite these manish shoes," she said to herself.

Sarah knew the Haighs, but she hadn't as yet met several of the other missionaries at Djoko Punda. She knew there were three missionaries from Sweden: Oskar Andersson, Elsa Lundberg and Henning Karlsson.

"Maybe I will be able to speak to the Swedish missionaries in German," she mentioned to Brother Herr.

"I know that Oskar Andersson speaks German," Herr replied, "I think you'll find him a very likeable person."

Brothers Herr and Johnstone had told the group at Kalamba a few things about Brother Andersson, so in many ways Sarah felt as if she already knew him. She knew he would be staying on at Djoko Punda while the Haighs were in the United States on a much needed furlough. Sarah knew that Brother Andersson would be in charge of the Djoko Punda station and legal representative of the mission there. Sarah also felt the responsibility she had been given to be the superintendent, secretary and official representative of the entire field during the absence of the Haighs. Sarah was grateful to know that Oskar Andersson would be her back-up person in these responsibilities. She had heard that he was very fluent in the French language. This would help.

The caravan with Sarah and the others was nearing Djoko Punda. Sarah noticed again the thick vegetation near the river that she remembered. Monkeys chattered nearby and drums sounded in the distance. This was the Africa she had learned to love those first few months she had been here even if the time had been very difficult with deaths and disturbances.

The paths the caravan had traveled included waist high grasses, open spaces, deep ravines and small bushes and trees. At one point the Africans had carried Sarah high above a deep stream on the top of a box. She was quite thin from losing much weight through illnesses, the change of food and hard work.

They had all looked out for animals and one antelope was seen, but most stayed a distance from their caravan.

Now the foliage was becoming dense. Umbrella trees, palm trees,

African mahogany and other varieties were noted.

Sarah straightened her dress, pushed back wisps of hair that had come undone beneath her helmet in the travels. Her shoes were dusty and muddy and still hurt her feet. She remembered their previous owner, Brother Stevenson.

"I will pay my respects at Stevenson's grave a bit later," she mentioned to Herr. "Right now I see the brickyard you told me about."

Chapter 20: Oskar Meets Sarah

"For the first time I saw Miss Kroeker who will now stay here
during the time the Haighs will be away on their furlough."
Diary of Oskar Andersson

April 26, 1915 began as usual for Oskar. Shortly before, Oskar had
begun to again fire the brick kiln. In order to safeguard the process he had
to live in the jungle beach tent days and nights for most of a week. Business
could be accomplished in between. News about some money on its way
from Sweden was a welcome report.

"Come, come," one of the fellow workers called. "A caravan has
arrived from Kalamba."

When Oskar came to where the group had gathered, he welcomed
Brother Herr warmly. Then he turned as he was being introduced to the
missionary who would be on their station during the Haighs' absence. He
had heard about this woman's nursing talents and courage in tense situa-
tions. And he couldn't help but notice her unusual manly shoes. The rest of
her was very womanly, however. He noted her dark wavy hair, her tall
form, her smile.

To those standing around, watching the introduction of Oskar
Andersson to Sarah Kroeker, it merely looked like any proper introduction
of a gentleman to a lady.

But Oskar would later relate to others, "It was love at sight in spite of
the mannish shoes."[1]

The group said goodbye to Oskar and continued their way up the hill to the mission station. About halfway up the hill the vines and underbrush were cleared and a cluster of huts and sheds revealed the Djoko Punda station. Most of the buildings were still made of mud and sticks with grass roofs. But some things had changed since Sarah had been here before. She noticed the layout of a new building.

"That must be the start of the new brick building you told me about," Sarah mentioned to Brother Herr as she adjusted her sun helmet.

"Yes, this building will be the first result of the brick making progress."

Sarah remembered the first huts: a dining room, a bedroom, a hen house and a store house.

May began with a memorable Sunday morning worship service for all those at Djoko Punda. Five persons stood up and said they wanted to follow Jesus in their lives. One of them was the first woman convert at Djoko Punda.

During Sunday school that day the Haighs gave farewell talks. On Friday, May 7, both blacks and whites trekked to the river to bid farewell to the Haigh family, the pioneers who were departing for their much needed furlough.

In his dairy Oskar wrote, "So now we are only young folks here. The biggest responsibility has come to me....God help all of us!"[2]

Early one morning Oskar woke up realizing that he was now in charge of this station, and Miss Kroeker was superintendent, secretary and official representative of the whole field during the Haigh's furlough. "Miss Kroeker is a very intelligent woman," he said to himself with a slight grin. "I admire her very much."

Nevertheless, the first week was very difficult for Oskar. The workers gave him extra problems once they knew he was in charge. They seemed to be testing him at every turn. He spent extra time trying to get ideas from his house-boy who, of course, knew the African people better than he did.

Sunday added a little brightness to the tense situation. Oskar, now Sunday school superintendent, fulfilled this job for the first time. The day went better than Oskar expected. Other things on the station seemed to be going better also.

Chapter 21: Coffee and Caring

"We now even receive coffee in the afternoon."
Diary of Oskar Andersson

"Would you like to have Sunday dinner with us?" Sister Kroeker and Sister Lundberg asked of the station's three bachelors one Sunday after the morning services.

One by one they gladly accepted.

Sarah and Sister Lundberg waited patiently at their hut for the gentlemen to arrive.

Sarah looked around. They had put together the few dishes and tableware that they had found among their things or in the storeroom. Sister Lundberg had made a Swedish tea ring with the ingredients she could find. Flowers were placed in a tin can in the center of a table that would barely hold five. Fish, caught by an African helper, plus sweet potatoes and fresh fruit completed the Sunday dinner.

When the men arrived, all seemed to suddenly be a bit shy. Finally when all was ready, Oskar seated Sarah, and Brothers Herr and Karlsson both went together to seat Sister Lundberg. This made everyone laugh and soon all were talking in mixed languages.

To the men's delight the women invited them to quit their cooking altogether and have their regular meals with them. What a change this was from the food the men and their helpers had been cooking.

By Saturday evening the group of young persons even felt that a party was in order. They invited Mr. Blommert from the government post to be their guest. Coffee, cake and fruits were served. Croquet was played.

Work continued on the station as usual, however. Services, outreach, school teaching, medical work, learning languages, brickmaking and building were still part of the routine. But a more pleasant climate seemed to prevail.

Illness continued to leave its mark as it had in the past. One by one and even several at once needed the care of Sarah and her nurse's training.

One afternoon Sarah needed a change of pace so she brought coffee to each of the bachelors where they were working. From then on the two women provided this afternoon treat each working day. Oskar especially liked it when it was Sarah's turn.

Wiping his brow from the sweat and smacking at the mosquitos, Oskar thought he heard voices. He paused in his task of walling in a firing place for the kiln. Turning around he glimpsed Sister Kroeker and Sister Lundberg coming up the path. His stomach gave a pleasant lurch. This time it wasn't indigestion. And it wasn't just the coffee time.

"We had a few extra hours so we thought we would like to see how this whole operation works instead of just a bit of it," Sister Kroeker commented, swatting a mosquito that had landed on her arm.

"I'd be happy to show you what we do here," Oskar replied, pleased with their extra attention to his work.

Oskar showed them around the operation, explaining about the first failed bricks, the new better clay and the watchfulness it took to keep things running smoothly. He didn't tell them about the heat, the mosquitoes and the night creatures. They could figure that out for themselves.

Now Oskar's main job, besides business and language study, seemed to be brick making. Oskar consulted with a visiting brick-layer at the government post for suggestions. After talking to him he felt that their operation at Djoko Punda had been doing quite well. But Oskar's body was not doing as well. Late in May Oskar began to again have very high fevers.

Sarah began to use her nursing skills to care for him during the times when he was very sick. She didn't want to have the same thing happen to him that happened to Brother Stevenson when she first arrived. Sarah had to admit she was beginning to like this Swedish missionary with his skills and his sense of humor. And he certainly was handsome! She better not let her feelings get in the way of God's will. Much prayer had been said about this, but what did Oskar think of her?

One night when Oskar was feeling well enough to write, he chronicled in his diary, "Miss Kroeker, who is a trained nurse, has from the beginning taken care of me so well that mamma could not have done it better."[1]

Oskar also noticed other things about this Miss Kroeker. To him she was very pleasing to look at even though others might think her plain. Quite often these days he would think of her.

She seemed to also have gifts of communication, teaching and leading the Sunday services when it was her turn. And she found such joy in her faith. Sarah mentioned at times that she hoped to see all her newfound black friends in heaven when it was her time to be there. Meanwhile here on earth Oskar wondered what Sarah thought of him.

Chapter 22: The Promise

"...Miss Sara (sic) Kroeker and I had decided to give each
a promise to love and belong to each other for life."
Diary of Oskar Andersson

Oskar seemed to be getting weaker each day. He attempted to do his tasks and studies, but finally his body gave out. His fever was 103 when he finally decided to go to bed once again and see if this might help.

Pots of hot water were placed around him. Blankets were placed on top of him. This, called the sweat bath, was still the preferred treatment for high fevers.

Sarah, now becoming a dear friend of Oskar, used her nursing skills to keep him as comfortable as possible.

During these long hours of contact with each other Oskar and Sarah were beginning to realize they truly wanted more than a worker-to-worker relationship.

One evening Oskar said to Sarah, his face almost in a smile despite his discomfort, "Do you think a German speaking Mennonite from America and a Swedish Christian could get along for life?"

Sarah smiled back. "I think their relatives and friends might have more of a problem with it than they would."

"And I guess both would have to learn each others' native language," Oskar commented with his sly sense of humor coming out despite illness. "And besides they need a married couple here."

As each examined their love and possible commitment it seemed almost impossible. Different cultural backgrounds. Different countries of origin. Different denominational backgrounds. Different languages. She didn't believe in killing. He came from a family of soldiers. She liked *plümemooss* and *zwiebach* and he liked fruit soups and tea rings.

What they had in common was their love for Christ, their commitment to serve Him, their love of Africans, Africa, and last but not least, their growing love for each other.

By June 3, Oskar's high fever was finally over. He seemed recovered, or at least improved for now. During the illness the love between the two increased despite communication gaps at times. German became their common language. Sarah had learned this in her Mennonite home and church. Oskar knew it enough to converse with her. Sometimes only their eyes did the talking.

One evening when the two were alone Oskar asked, "Sarah, would you and I be able to belong to each other for life? I know I should ask your father's permission, but we are too far away for that. I will write him if you accept."

Sarah's reply was quick. "I am willing with God's help."

Others on the station soon learned of Oskar and Sarah's intention to marry. Shortly thereafter a Thursday evening French lesson started as usual. But it ended on a different note.

"Surprise," the friends on the station announced. Then they shared the makings of a small cake and coffee party to celebrate the engagement of these two of their fellow workers.

"How many goats will you have to pay her father for the bride price? I remember when one chief offered about eight cows for her," Brother Herr mentioned. With that Sarah laughed remembering the incident that had occurred shortly after her arrival.

"I think she's worth at least nine goats," Oskar answered with a twinkle in his eyes.

Oskar also turned to the others and said, "I wonder who'll be next." He seemed to be looking in the direction of Brother Karlsson and Sister Lundberg who appeared to be enjoying each other's company more and more these days.

That night Oskar knelt by his cot and prayed, "Dear God, in your hands rest our lives and our ways! You are our strength."

On the next Saturday, Oskar and Sarah sat next to each other on a rough hewn table and wrote letters to family members and the mission committee in America telling of their planned marriage.

Official papers and legalities of various kinds would all have to be filled out and cleared before they could become one, but for now they were content. Even the station's black workers noticed a new cheerfulness in Oskar despite his recent illness.

Chapter 23: Relationships and Relaxation

"...and if Sara had not helped me so well it
would not be possible."
Diary of Oskar Andersson

Mission personnel differences and bouts with illnesses clouded the young couple's happiness. Nevertheless Sarah and Oskar studied Tshiluba together, and Sarah helped Oskar with his German. One respite was taking walks together.

"Let's plan our future garden," Oskar suggested one bright day as he brushed the insects away from his face.

"Maybe we should start with the foods the Africans plant such as yams and corn," Sarah mentioned.

"Then maybe we could try green beans, cucumbers, tomatoes and spinach to vary our diet," Oskar added. "But we'll have to do something to enrich the soil."

On June 3rd Sarah spoke at the morning services. Oskar was so proud of her. She seemed to be such a capable speaker even with the language differences.

Oskar used his French in many of the business matters.

Now if only the love and companionship they felt for each other could spread throughout the stations and across to the board in America.

Missionary differences continued, but the mission work itself progressed. Languages, backgrounds and views of Christian practices caused disagreements at times. Much discussion, prayer and concern was spent to work through various issues such as speaking in tongues, divine healing and just ordinary everyday relations. Finally, Oskar and Sarah felt peace in the relationships at their station.

Services, school, language study and building continued. The routine was broken by an all day prayer and testimony meeting for all the Christians on the station, both black and white. This was a first meeting of its kind at Djoko Punda. The mission staff also realized that they needed some time for rest and relaxation.

One fine June day the entire Djoko Punda staff paddled two canoes to Wissman Falls, a two hour or longer trip through rapids. Sometimes their canoes headed in the return direction despite their best efforts. Finally the group arrived at the falls. There they watched the local Africans fish. Muscular Africans had stretched vines across the falls. On these were hung huge, cone shaped baskets. The fish swimming in the large end were caught when trying to swim out the narrow end. In this way the Africans, deftly walking through the rapids, would catch large carp and catfish.

The group then bought fish from these local fishermen and had an excellent picnic and fellowship with the new African friends. The bananas and rolls they had brought along rounded out the meal.

Going home was easier, and a cup of hot coffee at the brickyard was a welcome treat on their return.

To keep everyone on the station informed of world events Oskar reported to them the world news he read in his Swedish newspapers. Most of the news was quite outdated by the time of the periodical's arrival, but no one knew any additional information so no one seemed to mind.

At the same time that Oskar and Sarah were courting there were two other courtships taking place. One couple was Brother Karlsson and Sister Lundberg and the other was Oskar's house-boy, Bukasa and Sister Lundberg's house-maid, Babutukabu.

One day Bukasa came to Oskar to ask if he could marry Babutukabu. After careful and prayerful consideration Oskar suggested they wait a little while longer and then they would be able to marry. Oskar felt that they needed to mature a bit in age and in their Christian lives. Oskar also knew that he would have to help provide the bride price to the girl's father since Bukasa was working for him.

Chapter 24: Wailing and Wedding Plans

"Had a letter from Dr. Morrisson in Luebo saying
that after much arrangement it is ready for us
to come over to be married."
Diary of Oskar Andersson

"Badibanga. Badibanga," cried one of the school boys as he rushed in to where Oskar was getting a much needed rest. Oskar jumped up and followed the boy to the river where a crowd had already gathered. The group pointed to the pile of clothes belonging to Badibanga, then out to the river.

Finally, Oskar was able to piece together the story. Four of the evangelist students had gone down to bathe in the river. Two of them had gone too far out, but the third, who could swim, saved both of them. When the three came up they looked around for the fourth, Badibanga. He was nowhere to be found! They feared he had slipped into the depths of the river or that a crocodile had taken him.

The rest of the afternoon, crying and wailing continued. That evening, at the Africans' request, a service was held by the river.

Patuamonangana ku makasa a Yesu, the group sang, (When we meet at Jesus' feet). The words of resurrection were then read from the Bible. Friends of Badibanga reported, "On the way to the river to bathe Badibanga had sung, "There is no friend like Jesus."

The next day Badibanga's body was found. His friends put clothes on him and wrapped him up. They dug the grave in a quiet way. In the evening a big crowd gathered near the open grave for a Christian burial service. According to those attending, God's Spirit seemed to be powerfully near.

It was customary in the villages near Djoko Punda that no one dared to go near the body except the closest relatives. The mother herself must dig the grave. This time many helped.

The presence of God's Spirit seemed to affect the workers and the work for the next few days. Persons were calm and cooperative.

Combining American and Swedish customs, both birthdays and name days were celebrated for Oskar and Sarah. July 19 was Sarah's day on the Swedish calendar so the station staff were up early to congratulate her with coffee and flowers.

Sweat poured from Oskar's body as he spent time in the tent by the river watching the kiln. Rodger, his faithful dog, kept him company and offered some protection. Sometimes the unexpected rain, coming in the dry season, would destroy the standing bricks.

While at the brickyard Oskar would study the languages he was trying to learn, pray for the work and what his own future would entail, and look forward to marriage with his beloved Sarah.

Occasionally Sarah, with other mission personnel, would show up for an impromptu visit. One day several came with some news. "Two more missionaries will be coming soon, a Mr. Tollefsen from Norway and a Mr. Edgardh from Sweden."

One Sunday evening all the mission personnel gathered on the beach for a prayer meeting. The stars shown in all their glory. Of course in all this beauty of the thick vines, large trees and glistening river, mosquitos and flies made themselves known.

On August 14, Oskar wrote in his diary, "Today it has been exactly one year since I arrived here. Much light and much darkness, but in everything the Lord has been my help and my strength."[1]

The women missionaries delighted the male missionaries by presenting them with new trousers they had sewn for each one. Oskar added to his diary, "When we in friendship can help each other, life even out here becomes a great pleasure — a paradise."[2]

But this paradise still included illness. Sarah became sick with a high fever and went to bed. While she was ill Sister Lundberg brought her some good news. "Your marriage papers are in order. You can go to Luebo to prepare for your wedding."

The same good news came to Oskar. When Oskar and Sarah finally had time to discuss the wedding plans they felt that Sarah should go on ahead to Luebo on a company boat. This of course would be only as soon as she felt well enough to undertake the trip. Oskar would follow when mission duties allowed and the official date was set. Sometime in September was the tentative date given.

Noises at the river indicated a company boat had arrived and it would be time for Sarah to depart for Luebo. The twosome said fond farewells, and Sarah reassured Oskar that she was well enough to make the trip.

Porters carried the extra supplies Sarah would need for their wedding to the waiting boat. The wedding would be simple but both felt they wanted it to be special in a Godly beautiful way.

Oskar trudged back to the kiln; his heart was with Sarah. But he knew the wait would be short, or so he hoped. One never knew, however, when legal papers and several countries were involved.

The hot, sweaty brick kiln was only part of the work for all those remaining on the station including Oskar. Business now included much work on justice issues between Africans and between Africans and the white government and business officials.

Oskar waved the official paper excitedly as he found out the wedding date had finally been set. "It has come!" he called to anyone within hearing distance. "It will be September 14!"

All was not peaceful on the station, however. One day the school boys came running.

"Muambi, muambi, lua, lua!" ("Preacher, preacher, come, come!")

When Oskar followed the school boys he found out that one of the other school boys had been shot and killed with an arrow by another African. When Oskar checked into it he found out that the shooting was supposedly accidental. An arrow aimed at a hen hit a tree and angled off hitting the boy by mistake.

Oskar and some helpers locked the culprit in a store room until Oskar could take him to Luebo for the government to deal with the situation.

The relatives of the dead boy wanted to bury the man who shot the arrow together with the dead boy as was the local African custom.

Early the next morning the prisoner escaped, fleeing in fear for his life from all parties. Nevertheless, he was caught in a village and returned to custody.

"When will I ever get to go to Luebo?" Oskar wondered. Prisoner problems and money problems at the mission both delayed his trip. Not enough funds seemed to be arriving from the United States for the regular work of the mission. Since he was in charge of Djoko Punda he felt the weight of these issues.

Chapter 25: Oskar Joins Sarah

"The first one I saw was my own friend Sarah. She looks so fresh and happy, we were so glad to see each other again."
Diary of Oskar Andersson

Finally, the day came when Oskar was able to start the journey toward Luebo for his wedding. Included in his caravan was the prisoner to be taken to the government officials.

The caravan settled for the night in Kadinga's village. Fine weather accompanied the caravan. Porters pointed out sights along the way.

4:30 a.m. was the starting time for the second day's trip. One stop was made in Kasangisha's large village. The Africans listened attentively as Oskar gave his own testimony. Some Catholic teachers attempted to disturb the meeting but ran away when Oskar began to pray.

Makaku's village was the next stop for the caravan. Here the group ate a hearty dinner and Oskar took careful pains to refresh himself from the travel dust and dirt. He wanted to be especially well groomed for his meeting with Sarah and other friends at Luebo.

Sarah looked well and happy when Oskar saw her. It seemed her stay at Luebo had refreshed her. They wanted to run to each other and embrace, but because of all the others looking on, their eyes had to tell their love. Both were so glad to see each other again!

When they found time to be alone they warmly embraced each other.

"I've missed you," Sarah stated brushing Oskar's mustache with her fingers.

"You looked so happy when I saw you, I thought maybe you had forgotten about me," Oskar replied, his eyes twinkling.

"Never! God has brought us together, and I know it will be for our lifetimes, and I hope that's a long time. By the way, have you been well?"

"Yes, thanks to God."

Payment of mission taxes, signing of wedding documents, dinners and photographs followed for the eager couple.

In between all the special events, some in their honor, Oskar took time to observe the hospital procedures, especially Dr. Stixrud performing operations.

Even the anticipated wedding couldn't keep Oskar from touring the Luebo brickyard and the construction work in progress. In his mind he was always comparing it to the procedures that were used at Djoko Punda.

"I don't think the bricks here are as good as the ones at our station," he told Sarah one afternoon. She just grinned.

Sunday came at Luebo with the morning service once again crowded with people. The afternoon Sunday school and evening mission staff meeting followed. Oskar was asked to teach a Sunday school class and lead the evening meeting. Sarah continued to feel pride in the many talents of her future husband but she kept these thoughts to herself. Growing up as a Mennonite in America she had been taught that pride was wrong. Mennonites attempted to be humble before God, but it wasn't always easy.

During their conversations with other missionaries they continued to hear of injustices against the Africans by many of the government and company men. Oskar and Sarah repeatedly heard of one man by the name of Sjöblom who had dared to protest these injustices. Even some missionaries did not back him.

Dr. Morrison, however, stated, "I had the best impression of him and remember him very well."

Once again, even amid the activities, Oskar and Sarah found time to be alone on walks and when letters needed to be written.

Occasionally the station personnel found some extra time to play the game of croquet which almost everyone seemed to enjoy. Even at this they had to watch for unwelcome visitors such as insects and snakes.

Chapter 26: The Wedding Day

*"Thanks to God for the clever and good helper You
gave me. God help us to be help and joy to each
other and to the glory of Your name!"*
Diary of Oskar Andersson

Sarah stood before the small mirror and observed her wedding attire. It was September 14, 1915. She would always remember this special date. She had put on a long, pale dress with a high collar edged in lace. She carefully placed a brooch at the collar of her dress. Sarah loved jewelry, and on this her wedding day she felt it was appropriate.

It took her a little while to get her hair just right with the veil and wreath of flowers. Soon it looked fine to her and she smiled at the reflection. This was her wedding day to her beloved Oskar.

Homesick thoughts intruded on her happiness. She so wished someone from her family or Oskar's family could be here to celebrate this important occasion with them.

She looked down at her shoes. This time she was wearing woman's shoes, white ones at that. "Funny that he loved me despite those men's shoes I used to wear."

Oskar carefully trimmed his mustache, bathed thoroughly and put on an all white suit and tie for the occasion.

"The only thing I miss today is having some of my family here or some of Sarah's. How they would enjoy seeing my wedding and meeting Sarah.

I know they will love her when they meet her."

Finally it was time for the official ceremony.

Accompanied by Dr. Morrison and Mr. James Allen, Oskar and Sarah went to the government post. Here the local official, Captain Bastin, married them using the French language.

Sarah didn't understand much of what was said but answered "*Oui, monsieur*," at the appropriate places.

The Faubert family on the station had previously invited Oskar and Sarah to come to their house for coffee after the civil ceremony. Here they enjoyed a few moments of relaxation before the next more festive event.

Sarah and Oskar walked hand in hand to the next stop of their special day. This was the home of Mr. Allen where they had been eating their meals since arriving at Luebo. Here they proceeded through a Christian wedding ceremony with Dr. Morrison in charge. This ceremony was more to Oskar and Sarah's liking than the official one. Dr. Stixrud led Oskar in and Miss Elda May Fair was Sarah's attendant. Sarah carried a bouquet of native flowers. More than twenty persons crowded the room for the happy event.

After the ceremony the guests gathered around a flower decorated table for refreshments which included cake, coffee and available fruits such as pineapple, papaya, bananas and oranges. Some of these had been planted by the mission staff.

Oskar was called upon to make a speech in both English and French. He appeared very elegant to Sarah in his white suit and tie. He made his speech to the assembled guests but once again his eyes spoke to Sarah.

While it was still daylight they posed for a wedding picture, both in white with Sarah carrying a lily bouquet.

Oskar and Sarah spent the first night of their marriage in the best accommodations the mission personnel at Luebo lovingly offered them. The excitement and beauty of the wedding day was over. Their life together was only beginning.

To begin this life they knelt beside their bed and once again offered their lives to each other and to the Lord who had led them together.

The honeymoon they had planned was to travel home by caravan to Djoko Punda with mission stops enroute.

Chapter 27: The Honeymoon Journey

"It is so easy and so quickly arranged now when I have a good wife with me on the trip. She arranges the food while I look after the bearers and arrange the tent and our other things."
Diary of Oskar Andersson

Oskar organized the bearers and supplies being sent back to Djoko Punda while Sarah planned the food items and supplies they would need for their honeymoon journey. After a final dinner at Luebo the couple and caravan began the trip.

Heavy rains made for an earlier stop for their second night of marriage. A company post provided an oasis with the official generously locating an empty house for them. He deftly arranged a bed. Grateful for this unexpected treatment the couple expressed their thanks to him.

The rain poured down in torrents. Oskar and Sarah knelt down by the bed together to say their prayers to God for the night and thanks again for the day past. Oskar reached over to help Sarah up and then drew her to him. Only a few leaks from the tin roof dampened their nightclothes.

Together they went to the bed the kind agent had prepared for them. Sarah's long, dark hair hung in waves and almost curls from the moisture. Even the dampness of the linens didn't deter their love.

The speed of the caravan porters was faster than their own speed as they continued travelling the next day. Most of the time their belongings were ahead of them. Somehow they were able to make do with what they had and what they were provided along the way.

Starting another day, they stopped at Chief Kasangisha's big village for a combination breakfast and noon meal. While there Oskar and Sarah ministered to the sick and held a meeting sharing the Gospel message of Christ after the village drum had announced the gathering.

At still another village, Chief Tshimbalanga's, their Gospel meeting was held by moonlight.

"A snake, a snake," one of the carriers yelled. That meeting was cut short as the Africans darted in all directions.

Less scary creatures were seen or heard on their journey. These were assorted birds that filled the air and surroundings with sound and color. The bulbul (nightingale) and the flappet lark were noted as were the doves, cuckoos and parrots.

The flowers and flowering bushes added their bright colors. The amaryllis were now gone, but the flame tree brightened the landscape with its clusters of red blossoms.

At another village stop they were able to gather a large, interested crowd. During the meeting, Ntumba, a Christian believer, sang to the gathered group. Ntumba had attended the Luebo mission school for several years. Her husband was also a Christian. Oskar and Sarah continued the meeting by showing some Sunday school pictures and telling the attentive crowd about Jesus.

The Africans loved the story of Jonah and the whale. Oskar and Sarah told the Africans, "We have both come far across the water to tell you about the one God who loves us and sent His Son to our world to save us from eternal punishment. But we have to turn from the worship of other gods and idols and ask God to forgive our sins. We must ask His spirit to come into our lives. His spirit is greater than any other spirit."

It would take time for the seeds of the gospel to be sown. This all seemed to be somewhat new to most of the Africans although a few had heard this before from those trained at Luebo.

"Look, Oskar, how beautifully they have decorated the station for us," exclaimed Sarah as they walked the final path to Djoko Punda. It was shortly after noon when they arrived.

Their friends at the station, not having been able to attend the wedding at Luebo, had prepared special festivities at the station. Brother Karlsson had just completed the floor in the new brick house so a welcome coffee was held there. Then the two special guests were escorted to a dinner at Sister Lundberg's.

Crates, satchels, baskets and their simple furniture were all moved into one small cottage on the Saturday following their arrival at Djoko Punda. As Oskar later wrote in his diary, "I am now living in a castle under a tin roof together with my Sarah."[1]

By Monday Oskar and Sarah were back to a more normal routine. An African boy was brought to them suffering from food poisoning. Together they revived him by rinsing his stomach.

Monday evening the Africans of the area were invited to a wedding banquet on the grass in honor of the marriage of Oskar and Sarah. Meat, beans, "bidia" and vegetables, which included elephant leaves, manioc leaves and pigweed, were happily consumed.

Mr. Thill, from the company post, brought them a finely crafted clock as a wedding present.

Brick making, keeping the accounts and other business duties kept Oskar busy. This included continually making decisions in palavers or disagreements among the Africans. Many times these were concerning chickens, goats or their work for the station.

Sarah continued with nursing duties, preparing for an evangelistic trip to outlying villages and taking her turn at preaching. Her turn came Sunday, September 26, just shortly after their marriage. Oskar led the Sunday school that same Sunday.

"We'd better sit down and write to both of our parents today, as they will want to hear all the news of the wedding," Oskar said to Sarah that afternoon between services.

That night they prepared their heads and hearts for the first long outreach trip they would take together as husband and wife, not including their honeymoon trip from Luebo.

Together they knelt in prayer.

Oskar started: "Lord guide our trip. Keep the evil one from putting blocks in our way as we try to reach our friends for Christ. Keep us all safe from diseases and the more dangerous creatures. In Jesus name. Amen."

Then Sarah added, "Help our hands to heal those we meet. And assist us as we try to lead them to Jesus, our beloved Savior, so we can all meet at Jesus feet someday. In Jesus name we pray, Amen."

Chapter 28: Outreach Adventures

*"We slept in a house, the 'hostel'. Here are hundreds of rats
who examined all our things and created a terrible noise."*
Diary of Oskar Andersson

The birds made their morning sounds. The palm branches waved in the breeze. Oskar and Sarah rose early on Monday morning to pack their bed rolls, clothing, food, medical supplies, photographic equipment and evangelistic materials that they had assembled to be ready for the caravan of porters.

Finally they were all packed and prepared to visit the outlying villages with hopes of treating the sick, telling Africans about Christ and possibly bringing back some students for the school.

The caravan started off with the blessings of the remaining staff and workers. The deftness of the African porters once again amazed the two as they traveled. Part of the time they were carried in hammocks and part of the time they walked. The porters chanted or sang as they trekked.

A highly interested group met them at Chief Ndombe's village that evening. Oskar and Sarah continued the usual routine of first treating the sick and then holding a service.

Another highly interested group met them that night when they tried to sleep in a "hostel", a mud and thatch hut built to shelter government officials. This group consisted of hundreds of rats. Suddenly Sarah screamed! A rat had landed on her face despite the mosquito netting and other precautions.

"I'll light a lamp and see if that will keep them away," Oskar exclaimed, shooing the rats away with his feet and hands. He then checked to see if Sarah was bitten. Gladly he noted that the netting had prevented this. The two didn't sleep much that night, especially Oskar who kept watch.

"Bamama," (Mothers) the women and children called respectfully as they ran out to meet Oskar and Sarah at each village. They were happy to see a missionary woman. They expected women to be different from the government officials and other men in power they had known.

"How good this feels to be clean again," Sarah remarked after warm water for a bath was provided for them at the village of Chief Tshimpangu. Here they were also provided a good dinner, African style.

After these amenities they were ready for a service at another village, that of Chief Bakombula.

The Africans sat around the fire where they gathered for other stories and dances. A drum announced the gathering.

After Sarah and Oskar had treated all those they could, the service began. Tonight the injuries had included an infected knife wound, several children with high fevers and others who just wanted to see and taste the white man's medicine.

First Oskar told the story of Daniel in the lion's den with card pictures. He told how God had protected Daniel because of his faith and prayers. Then Sarah told how Jesus had died on the cross for all persons, black and white.

Oskar ended with an invitation for them to ask God to forgive their sins and to trust the one true God.

"Do we have to give up our other gods?"

"Yes," replied Oskar kindly, "but this one God will be all you need."

"Will the evil spirits get us?" another asked.

"Not if you trust in the true spirit of this one God."

It seemed that tonight the goats, babies, chickens and youngsters were noisy but the people were listening and asking questions. Sometimes it was difficult for Oskar and Sarah to understand. At times their porters helped them in translation.

When the meeting was just about concluded several Africans brought a man who was very ill from crocodile wounds. Sarah cleaned the wounds, gave him some medicine and found some assorted thread to sew up the wounds. Her white thread was all used up quickly.

"We will come back here in some days and remove the stitches," she tried to explain. "But don't take him to any witch doctors. We will pray that his wounds will heal."

Finally Oskar and Sarah sat down to what they thought would be a relaxing meal. Suddenly swarms of ants attacked them. The couple made a hasty exit. These were flying ants which often made their way out of the mud walls. If they had been Africans they would have just enjoyed putting them in their mouths and chewing them while grabbing for others.

Next the exhausted couple settled down in their tent hoping for a restful night. Suddenly rain, wind, lightning and thunder arrived with a vengeance! The noise and wetness ruined their sleep, but the biggest fear was that their tent would also be demolished. Finally, just when the birds were beginning to awaken, Oskar and Sarah fell asleep. When they finally did wake up they were greatly relieved to note that their tent was not ruined. It just needed some stitching like the man with the crocodile wounds.

Rats, ants and rain did not stop their journey. Other villages were visited. At one village they treated a man with a fever of 105. At another, three boys joined their caravan to return with them to the mission school. Other villages also promised to send boys to the school. At every village, Bible passages in the local language were distributed.

Chiefs gave gifts such as eggs, hens, and even goats, expecting gifts in return. These return gifts from the missionaries included salt, cloth and Bible pictures.

Sometimes plodding, sometimes almost running, the caravan made its way through swamps and over high plateaus. At one village the people all ran to hide when they saw the caravan coming. When one of the village boys found out who they were, from the boys in their caravan, he began shouting, *"Bena Mission"* not *"Bula Matadi"* (government agent). Then the people returned to greet them.

Exhausted, but encouraged, and with a number of boys for the mission school, Sarah and Oskar returned to their home at Djoko Punda. What a welcome sight it was!

New jobs and additional challenges were waiting at the station.

Chapter 29: Changes and Challenges

*"Our dinner table was probably the biggest that had
ever been in Djoka (sic) Punda. Besides that we
are now eight persons here, we were visited by two
company men who also went with us to church."*
Diary of Oskar Andersson

When Oskar and Sarah arrived back at Djoko Punda, Oskar had several new responsibilities. A number of persons needed tooth extraction, a service which he provided. New roads also had to be planned. And meat was sorely needed for everyone's diet.

Oskar didn't mind helping with the latter two jobs, especially the hunting.

"We need meat to eat," Oskar explained to one of his African friends.

"I will show you where many monkeys live," the African replied. Sarah went along to check on their own forest garden.

When they came nearer the location the hunting party treaded softly and and hid behind trees and dense undergrowth.

Finally Oskar felt that he had just the right position. The shot rang through the dense forest, and monkeys scrambled away.

But there on the ground were two dead monkeys!

The Africans grinned at him. This white man was a good hunter.

Together they dressed the meat and carried it home.

"I killed two with just one shot," he proudly stated to Sarah who was glad for the meat, some of which he shared with his African guides.

"Your own praise stinks," she said with a grin. "That's an old Low German saying that my family sometimes used," she added. "But the meat doesn't, so I'm glad for that."

The food situation was also greatly helped when forty cases of supplies came from the United States. Much of this was food, some from Sarah's relatives.

Oskar continued with his medical studies, replanted trees and made a separate door in the church for latecomers. Each worship service had been greatly disturbed by the late arrival of many persons. This annoyed Oskar so much that he built the extra door where the latecomers could enter less noticeably.

In the services, converts gave testimonies and offered prayers. In their prayers they often said, "God, put the devil on the other side of the water and bind him there."[1]

Sarah was kept busy with nursing duties, especially the care of Sister Lundberg who became seriously ill.

At times the fellow missionaries thought Miss Lundberg might not make it. At one point she went into convulsions and became unconscious for some time. When she came to she said, "Oh how it is light and beautiful. I am going home."[2]

Finally, after much prayer and continued nursing, Sister Lundberg rallied. The group felt that a miracle of divine healing had taken place.

For a brief time the dinner table at Djoko Punda included eight persons. First there were the five already in place: Oskar and Sarah, Sister Lundberg, Brother Karlsson and Brother Herr. Three new workers had joined the staff: Brother Tollefsen from Norway, Brother Edgardh from Sweden and also Sister Karlsson from Sweden.

This large group was shortlived however. Brother Karlsson and Sister Lundberg left for Kalamba. Brother Herr, who for some time had a strained relationship with the mission's leader, Brother Haigh, was to leave the

Congo work altogether. Sarah had known him from her very early days with the mission.

On November 29, 1915, Oskar had a very important task. He carefully wrote the official business letter for the purchase of the Djoko Punda station grounds.

Oskar had another important and pleasant task. Bukasa, Oskar's house servant, once again asked if he could marry Bakutukabu, a house girl of the station. Oskar gave his permission and then was partially responsible for paying the bride price.

The bride price was 40 pieces of cloth or 200 francs. Oskar helped with the payment even though he thought the bride's family, was asking a bit too much.

This same Bukasa came privately to Oskar and stated, "I want to be an evangelist to my people. Can you help me?"

"Yes," Oskar replied, pleased with the request. "I will help you all I can."

Mission personnel relationships were still strained at times. Oskar waited and waited for directives from the board in the United States. Finally, one longed-for letter arrived with instructions. He felt now he had some backing in decisions.

Routine continued. Workers received wages and made purchases. Oskar and Brother Edgardh braved a village trip. Oskar employed the use of a projector which the Africans enjoyed.

At one village the two arrived in the middle of the afternoon. The sun was causing sweat to pour from their bodies. Suddenly out of nowhere Africans surrounded them with loaded rifles.

Oskar stepped forward, his knees shaking, his heart beating and more sweat pouring from his body.

"Bena Mission," he tried to say so all could hear.

Immediately some of his African porters stepped forward with him to help explain.

"They are here to bring good medicine and good stories."

Finally, but slowly, the village Africans put down their rifles and led the group to the chief's hut. Drums sounded.

After this experience the remainder of the trip was much less traumatic. Oskar appreciated the company of Brother Edgardh. Following the services and medical assistance to the Africans, the two had times of chatting about their homeland. It helped ease the homesickness that each felt.

Chapter 30: New Year, New Son, New House

"Kusa was a poor, sick, negro slave. He was pushed away
from his village in order to die in the forest. Half dead,
with his body full of sores, he found the way to us.
My wife helped him, and he is now her foster son."
Diary of Oskar Andersson

Finally Christmas arrived! The previous year Oskar had been somewhat disappointed in the type of Christmas activities. The rainy weather had also dampened the spirits considerably. This year he tried to combine the traditions and cultures of all the persons on the station. And he had a wife to ease his loneliness!

The station personnel had a party with a palm tree taking the place of a Christmas tree. When Christmas morning arrived a service was held for everyone. This time the weather was cooperative. Palm branches decorated the grass church. Oskar brought a message about the birth of the Savior. Even the men from the Compagnie du Kasai (rubber company) came to the service.

Then blacks and whites gathered for contests, races and other games with prizes as they had done the previous Christmas. As a Christmas gift each worker received a new shirt. Each person who took part in the games received a large red handkerchief.

As the New Year began Oskar and others were busy finishing the new, more permanent, brick house. Oskar also continued as head of the station, tradesman, Sunday school teacher and evangelist. One problem he encountered was with discipline in the Sunday school.

Sarah was in charge of the regular school with the help of Brother Edgardh. She also started a nursing school and added the evangelist's school to her agenda.

In the latter part of January, Kusa, a poor, sick, black slave came to the station begging for help. He had been pushed away from his own village in order to die in the forest. Half dead and full of sores, he found his way to the mission station.

Sarah nursed him back to health and soon took him under her wing as a "foster" son. After all her care, and when Kusa was well, the owner tried to get him back. He was unsuccessful!

In early February another change took place on the station. Sister Karlsson left for Luebo to work with the Presbyterians. This left only four persons on the Djoko Punda station to perform all the needed tasks. Oskar and Sarah, Brother Tolefssen and Brother Edgardh were now the entire staff.

Work was interrupted in March by two simple birthday celebrations: coffee, cake and a few flowers given. Sarah's birthday was on March 13 and Oskar's was on March 21. On Sarah's birthday Oskar laid floors in the new brick house, and on his birthday Oskar erected walls.

A whistle from the river indicated that the government steamer had arrived. The mail that it brought was an additional treat for Oskar and Sarah and welcome news for the others.

On April 3, Oskar came in to Sarah with happy news. The brick house was now ready for occupancy. Of course there was also work to be done on other buildings. The ceiling in their old room was torn down and replaced to prepare it for the Haighs when they would complete their furlough.

Sarah had already planted roses and other flowers outside the new residence in preparation for the moving in event. A braided rug was hung on the wall of the dining room for decoration.

Happily Oskar and Sarah, with helpers, carried their modest belongings to the new sturdy brick house.

"Sarah, look what has arrived," Oskar joyfully announced one April day. "It is the new ra dioptika projector from America. Now I can show better pictures of the life of Jesus."

Sarah rejoiced with her husband as she knew what this would accomplish in their work with the Africans.

Chapter 31: Babies and Baking

"Before, we had a little monkey and two parrots.
Also we have a cat, but he is in the forest
most of the time."
Diary of Oskar Andersson

Sarah cuddled the little creature in her arms. It was a monkey that Oskar had found orphaned in the forest. Around her were the flowers she had planted before the new residence was completed. She kept a watchful eye on everything around her. Two poisonous snakes had recently tried to enter their new house. Oskar had killed both of them, much to Sarah's relief.

Sarah loved animals, except snakes. She loved babies, especially human babies. She loved helping to bring them into the world. Then she enjoyed teaching the mothers how to care for them in a loving, clean way.

As she cuddled the monkey she thought of giving it a name. "But what can I name a baby monkey? What can we name any baby? What can Oskar and I name the baby we will have some months from now?" Oskar was looking forward to being a father, and Sarah was eager to have her own baby. As yet no one else knew.

She was sick several mornings. But with malaria and other illnesses no one seemed to notice.

"I hate to think of what happens to the African babies that are not wanted by the parents," Sarah said to herself. She remembered the twins born where one had disappeared shortly after the birth. She also wondered what happened to the babies of African mothers and white government men. She knew she hadn't seen any mulatto children in the villages. A horrible thought crossed her mind. She thought of babies torn to pieces by animals in the forest or babies thrown into the river.

She gave the monkey a squeeze and went in search of the house boy, Bukasa. "You tie it up, I will feed it," she instructed him. "Make it stay here."

It seemed to Sarah that their yard was becoming like a small farm. Hens and ducks were walking about. A young dog, the son of Rodger, chased anything that moved. Their dozen goats were kept in a nearby village, and their household cat lived in the forest most of the time.

The next day when Sarah saw the baby monkey tied with a long rope to the large umbrella tree, she knew what she wanted to do. Now she would see that the monkey was fed like a newborn baby. But sometime in the future, she would find a way to save the babies that ended their lives in the forest. Even if she had to take care of them herself like she had with the black slave boy. First she would have to continue to win the trust and respect of the people around her.

Sarah wasn't feeling too well on the next Saturday morning. As far as she knew there were no medical emergencies or babies about to be born. But one never knew what might be needed in one of the villages. Her medical supply kit was packed in its black leather bag complete with bandages made from old bed linens.

All at once she heard their houseboy signal his arrival by a cough. She went to the door and tried out her Tsiluba. "*Lua,*" (Come). In he came with a large wooden crate. He was assisted by another worker.

Sarah was excited when she saw the crate. "This must be from my family in America!"

By now Oskar had also entered the house. "I think you're right, and it probably took at least six months to get here. Let me get my tools to open it carefully. Then we can use the wood to make furniture or storage cases."

After Oskar removed the lid, Sarah examined the contents. A small quilt was near the top. Then came tea towels made from flour sacks. Beneath these were cans of lard for cooking or baking.

Sarah was so happy to receive this box from her family that she sat in a chair and held the can of lard close to her heart. She knew it had been in the hands of ones she loved.

When the house boy left, Oskar smiled and said, "This crate is very sturdy. I think we'll use it to store things you sew now for our baby. We'll start by putting this quilt in it."

"Mama, Mama, *lua, lua*," the houseboy called running into their midst without the usual polite coughs at the door.

Sarah and Oskar followed and found one of Oskar's brick workers with a large stab wound on his arm. Two of the workers had gotten into a fight over a chicken, and one had managed to stab the other. The chicken had gotten away.

Sarah knew Oskar would punish the two by withholding some of the monthly pay of salt and cloth. Nevertheless she offered the injured worker some chicken broth, left from one of their meals, to help replace the blood lost.

"You must not try to get even," Sarah explained to the worker as best she could in his language. "That is not the Jesus way." In her mind she was worried what his family might do. Family members had been known to kill the person who injured a member of their family.

Sarah said to herself, "How much our black friends here need to learn about Christ and His love." Then she recalled some of the government and company men and their treatment of the native Africans. "They'll undo everything we're trying to teach here."

After making sure the worker was in a safe condition, Sarah returned to their home to try to use some of the lard she had just received. Her insides felt better now, and she was in the mood to do some baking.

Donning a large apron which covered most of her cotton dress, Sarah began the day long task of *zwieback* making. This was the low German double bread roll that was a favorite of her relatives in America. These Mennonite people had brought this recipe with them from South Russia when they migrated to America in the 1870s and 1880s.

"I think I'll also try to make Oskar something from his Swedish homeland too, that is if my stomach will stay settled long enough.

Sarah formed the little double rolls and set them aside for an additional rising. Her body wouldn't cooperate however. A wave of dread overcame her with some added nausea. "Is this normal nausea or is something else wrong with me?" She knew plenty about childbirth, maybe too much. But there was no other woman now on the station to talk to in order to see if this was normal. She tried to remember her mother's pregnancies, but suddenly she was too tired to even think.

Finally fatigue and nausea made Sarah lie down on the bed. She drifted into a fitful nap. "*Yesu,*" (Jesus), "*Nzambi,*" (God) she found herself saying over and over. Then it came out in German, English, then Swedish. She awoke with a start.

Was she becoming delirious? Did she have malaria? Would it harm the baby? She knew Oskar hadn't been feeling very well. Now was she going to be sick too? As if to conquer any disease or temporary illness by hard work, she set her mind and hands once again on the baking.

She put the *zwieback* in the brick oven and began to make some *plümemooss* (dried fruit pudding) for supper. Oskar would like this because it was very much like the fruit soups from his native Sweden. She was able to make this today because she had found some dried prunes and raisins in the crate from her family. She cooked the fruit and made a paste of flour, sugar and cinnamon with a little water. She gradually added this to the cooked fruit mixture and brought it to a boil. After about five minutes of stirring she set it aside to cool. Later she would add whatever milk or cream she could find, that is if there was enough left from their other meals.

By the time Oskar arrived from his other mission tasks at the storeroom and brickyard, Sarah was ready with the plümemooss and zwieback. He seemed unusually weary, but he ate the supper with delight. As he ate, he stated with a chuckle, "This low German, American, Swedish, Congo marriage is very nice."

Chapter 32: Working and Waiting

*"My wife preached in the morning for a crowded
house. The Lord made the word live."*
Diary of Oskar Andersson

Work at the mission station continued. Oskar was still involved in
supervising the brick making, studying, preaching and teaching. He was
also preparing for the return of the Haighs who were expected at any time.
Work on the buildings continued.

Sarah also studied the languages, did nursing duties and made their
household as inviting as possible with the items available. The new brick
house made many things much nicer. Sarah managed to do her share of
teaching and preaching.

Sometimes Oskar became very discouraged. Language differences, cultural differences, even various religious differences still made working
together difficult on the stations and with the board in America. The language barriers complicated the writing or discussion of these differences.
Once in a while Oskar discussed with Sarah the possibility of working in
another field in the Congo under Swedish direction. He had written some
letters of inquiry and received some answers in return.

Sarah and Oskar prayed continuously to ask God's guidance in all these
matters. Sometimes Sarah was homesick to see her family and to meet
Oskar's family.

"Will we have a chance to let our baby meet his or her grandparents?"

Sarah asked Oskar one day.

"Only the Lord knows," Oskar replied, "but I hope so."

In the latter part of April Sarah began taking Swedish lessons. Brother Edgardh was her teacher. Since Oskar and Sarah had been using German as their common language it hadn't been as crucial as it might have been in any other situation.

Africans gathered one evening for Oskar to use his new "cinema" from the United States, the "ra dioptika." It was larger and more powerful than his previous projector.

The Africans became so excited when they saw the first pictures of the life of Jesus that Oskar could hardly give an explanation.

Sometime later Oskar received a letter for which he had been anxiously waiting. He opened it carefully. "The Haighs are on their way back," he informed Sarah.

May 19 arrived and so did the government boat. On it were the Haighs. The Haighs were now again in charge of both the Djoko Punda station and the entire mission program.

Oskar and Sarah were pleased to see that three other missionaries from the United States were with them also: Mr. and Mrs. J. P. Barkman and Miss Agnes Sprunger. The Barkmans were happy to regularly have meals with Oskar and Sarah.

"How cheerful the Barkmans are," Oskar said to Sarah one day. "They are good company."

Despite the fact that they were good company new tensions arose with the additional persons on the field. The annual meeting of the whole mission was held. Differences still continued all around. Oskar and Brother Haigh engaged in extensive Christian dialogue with each other concerning such issues as support, speaking in tongues, divine healing, etc.

One issue was that the European missionaries did not receive support from the Congo Inland Mission in America except for the use of the station facilities and supplies. They had to procure their own support from individual homelands.

Through talking it over and much prayer and Christian love the two arrived at mutual understandings.

Mission assignments were made. The Barkmans, Brother Edgardh and Sister Sprunger. would go to Kalamba. Sister Lundberg would come back to Djoko Punda.

Once again Oskar's body didn't cooperate. His temperature went very high! Stomach pains increased. Sarah spent much time nursing him. Quinine helped somewhat. Hot poultices and enemas were tried. A dose of ipecacuanha was given. Oskar couldn't keep it down!

Sarah and Oskar both prayed intensely. Sarah felt that somehow she and Oskar were being tested or disciplined by the Lord.

"Why Lord, why?" she would pray. "Please heal him. Have we not been faithful to you?"

On June 14, all the missionaries on the station gathered to pray for him. Still no change. The evening of June 17 found Oskar and Sarah alone in the room. This had been his worst day.

Together they prayed as they had for some time. But this time Oskar felt the power of God overshadowing him. "Glory to His name, who makes miracles among His children,"[1] Oskar praised.

That evening was the turning point. By the following Monday Oskar was able to sit up.

Chapter 33: Sorrow

"At 2:30 the birth ended, but our little son was dead.
He had the umbilical cord around his neck and shoulder
and because of the prolonged birth he was suffocated."
Diary of Oskar Andersson

Oskar's health steadily improved with only a few minor setbacks.

On July 31st, Oskar and Sarah, with the Barkmans, boarded a steamer for Luebo. Oskar and Sarah were given this privilege because of the impending birth of their first child. They looked forward to this time at Luebo with the friends they had made there on the previous visit.

The captain of the steamer was from Sierra Leone and a Spanish gentleman was also aboard. At places the water was very low, but the ship never grounded.

"Isn't the tropical greenery beautiful?" Oskar pointed out to Sarah as they journeyed.

"This certainly isn't Texas, Kansas or Chicago," Sarah replied noting the palms, vines and flowering trees. African gray parrots were observed as were doves and cuckoo birds.

The steamer wasn't large enough for sleeping so the four from Djoko Punda erected a large tent on the shore each evening.

The captain and Spanish gentleman ate all their meals with the missionaries. It appeared by their thin bodies that they lacked food to eat, and the missionaries were glad to share the provisions they had packed.

A small group of missionaries welcomed them when they arrived at Luebo. The station was currently short of staff so Oskar and Sarah were given a whole house to live in for the duration of their stay.

Oskar and the Barkmans helped as best they could with various station responsibilities. Sarah, due to her condition, was allowed to rest more than usual, and she needed it. Even her body was telling the effects of the last weeks of pregnancy.

Sixteen persons, including the four from Djoko Punda, enjoyed a Saturday evening picnic. The evening included a game of croquet plus the joy of an African wedding.

On Sunday the Anderssons and Barkmans observed the baptism of 120 persons as Dr. William Morrison sprinkled the adults. 1500 adults and children attended the Sunday school with the Africans doing most of the work.

"Dr. Morrison," Oskar asked one day, "would you have some time to help us work through some details about our future?"

Oskar respected Dr. Morrison very much because he always had a warm heart for the Africans and tried to gain their rights with the government.

The three sat down at a crude wooden table and discussed all the pros and cons of staying with the Congo Inland Mission, starting new mission work under another group or going back to one of their homelands.

Oskar's health was a matter of concern. Various Christian views was another issue.

Later Oskar noted the calendar. It was August 14. He remarked to Sarah. "It has now been two years since I came to Djoko Punda and eleven months since our wedding."

Giving her a gentle hug around her ample body he added, "and God has blessed me with you and this child of ours."

Responding with a peck on the cheek, Sarah added, "And I have also been truly blessed ." Her thoughts were both in the present and in the past when she recalled how worried she had been when Oskar was so ill. She remembered pleading with God for Oskar's recovery.

A little nudge of worry crowded Sarah's mind when she remembered how she had prayed at one time. She had said, "Lord, if you must take one of us take the baby, because if Oskar dies no one from Sweden will ever want to work in missions in the Congo. And you know how much I need him too."

Sarah brushed that memory aside and proceeded with the day's activities.

Oskar continued to find jobs at Luebo to keep him occupied. With bricks and iron he completed the kitchen of the house where they were staying. Another day he helped to build an outhouse.

Croquet continued to be the evening relaxation for the station's staff. Each, however, was careful to watch for snakes.

Sarah and Oskar awoke on Saturday to the noise of voices and animals. "Oh, yes," Oskar said to Sarah, "I had forgotten, but today is market day here and thousands will be in the area to buy and sell."

Later that day members of the staff, including Oskar, toured the vendors, buying what was needed for the station as they bartered with the sellers. Baskets, beads, gourds, greens, eggs and live chickens shared space with mats, mortars and pestles.

Oskar seemed in better health each day although now and then his stomach didn't appear to be 100% well. Sarah's body slowed down to the pace of a woman awaiting the birth of a child.

One muggy day Oskar and Sarah followed the Barkmans to the river to say farewell. The Barkmans were to return to Djoko Punda and from there were to be transferred to Kalamba. It had been helpful for the Barkmans to observe the Presbyterian work at Luebo. And Oskar and Sarah had appreciated their company. Neither couple knew when they would see each other again, so the parting was bittersweet.

The everyday routine of the station was saddened by the death of the two month old baby of one of the Luebo missionary couples. Sarah felt for the parents and prayed concerning God's will for the baby moving within her. She noted each kick and move with joy.

One day Oskar reported to Sarah, "I will be going on an evangelistic trip with an African evangelist, Kabeya Lukenga. I have been told by other missionaries that none of the white men can be more important for the work here than he is."

"We need to do more of this working together, black with white," Sarah answered, feeling a strong kick within her womb.

The station's school started after what had been a two month vacation. Oskar was asked to supervise it with African teachers doing all the teaching. The school consisted of some fifty classes, so this job filled much of Oskar's time, but he still kept an eye on Sarah who he knew was nearing the time of birth.

On Sunday, September 10, Sarah woke abruptly. "Oskar, I felt some pains. I think the time is coming for our baby to be born. Then she paused. "But I don't think it will happen before afternoon or so." She was thinking back and remembering the long labors of most first time mothers she had known.

"Are you sure?" Oskar asked nervously. "Maybe I shouldn't go and hold the meeting in Kalamba's village."

"No, you go. They're so short of missionaries here. Just go first and get the missionary nurse to stay with me and tell Dr. Coppedge. I'll be in capable hands."

500 persons or more showed up at Kalamba's village for the service that morning, but Oskar felt anxious, so he hurried home as soon as possible. Sarah was glad to see Oskar when he arrived even though he seemed unusually nervous and breathless.

The pains were coming quickly, and Sarah clutched Oskar.

Dr. Coppedge and a nurse were also in the room. Dr. Coppedge considered that the pains were coming too quickly so he administered injections and chloroform in order to prolong the birth. What he gave took away the pains more than desired. He then compensated by giving Sarah a stimulant.

At 2:30 p.m. the birth ended, but the little one was not breathing. The umbilical cord was wrapped around the neck and shoulder, and the baby had suffocated! Frantically the three who were in the room, including Oskar, gave artificial respiration, but to no avail.

"He has gone home to God," Oskar whispered to Sarah lovingly as tears streamed down both their cheeks. Their gazes turned to the child and both noticed how handsome he appeared. With that they both wept long and hard after the nurse and doctor quietly left the room to give them moments of privacy.

"Will my Sarah be alright?" Oskar asked the doctor when he encountered him privately.

"She appears to be doing well under the circumstances, but we are so very sorry about your loss," the doctor replied, turning his face away so Oskar wouldn't see his own tears.

The little grave, with its low wall built by Oskar, marked the experience. The hearts of Sarah and Oskar bore the scars.

A few days later, on September 14, Oskar and Sarah, even in their sorrow, remembered that this was their first wedding anniversary. Oskar suggested they have devotions together, to remember their wedding day, as he handed her a fresh bouquet.

Sarah wiped tears from her eyes and consented.

"We both came here to serve the Lord and tell the Africans about Jesus. We can still do that after you get well, even though right now we wish things had turned out differently. Maybe God is trying to tell us something." Oskar said these words softly to Sarah after he had finished reading some verses of comfort and love.

Sarah was too tired to reply. She was suffering from milk fever. Oskar took her hand and prayed for both of them. "Dear Lord, we don't know why we have to go through this sorrow. We both wanted this baby so much. But only you know what is best for us and our service to you. Please heal Sarah and heal both of our hearts. In Jesus name we pray, Amen."

Oskar was worried about Sarah. He continued to pray for her healing. By September 17, Sarah was able to be at the dinner table, much to Oskar's relief.

Sarah continued to improve. So in appreciation for what the people at Luebo had done for them, Oskar and Sarah with the help of Sister Karlsson, formerly of Djoko Punda, gave a Swedish dinner for the whole station.

Fish, fruit soup and good Swedish coffee were included. A Swedish tea ring completed the meal. The best dishes and other tableware which could be found at Luebo were used.

"You will spoil us here," one of the guests proclaimed, "but we are very grateful to you for this event."

"We are the ones who are grateful to you," spoke Oskar.

Oskar entered the room where Sarah was slowly packing some of their belongings to be ready to return to Djoko Punda when a boat arrived to take them.

"The Domerys had a healthy baby today, Sarah."

Sarah paused in her packing. "I'm happy for them, but God help me not to be jealous."

"Maybe this will help cheer both of us. We've been invited to an African meal of *bidia* and peppered chicken at the MacElroys." Oskar tried to sound normal.

"These people here have been so good to us. If we ever again need a break from Djoko Punda, I know we would be welcome here." Sarah folded one more item and placed it in the satchel. "Oh, I think I will give the Domerys' baby some of the clothes I sewed for ours. If we have another, I can make some more." Tears wet her cheeks. Oskar took her in his arms. Soon she felt the dampness of his tears.

The day of departure from Luebo arrived. October 11, found them boarding a boat for Djoko Punda. Oskar had a feeling that sometime they might be returning to Luebo or another mission station, rather than Djoko Punda.

"Lord guide us," they prayed together.

Oskar and Sarah both hoped that some day they would have a live child of their own in their arms rather than returning empty armed as they were now. Sarah remembered the prayer she had prayed and was glad Oskar was still with her. Oskar was content that Sarah, his bride of one year, was well and strong.

Chapter 34: Farewell

"Already at 5:30 in the morning we were down at the boat.
All the natives were there to say farewell."
Diary of Oskar Andersson

At Dibanga, enroute home to Djoko Punda from Luebo, Oskar and Sarah accepted an invitation to be guests of Mr. Rusmont, a local government official. As fellow dinner guests they ate with two company agents who had traveled on the boat from Luebo.

In the dinner conversation that followed one of the men declared, "All the negroes must be poisoned or in another way be tortured to death!"[1]

Oskar, Sarah and Mr. Rusmont adamantly disagreed, but the agent didn't seem to understand or didn't care to.

When Sarah and Oskar were once again alone Sarah stated emphatically, "Maybe we're missionaries to the wrong people!"

"I don't know how they expect to have workers in their company with that attitude!" Oskar exclaimed. "Now I know I'll be more compassionate to our black brothers and sisters."

"We must continue to work in the Congo," Oskar added. "But first we'll take some time off and visit our countries."

Earlier Oskar had written in his diary, "May God through this make us bound fast to Africa and more devoted to Him!"[2] Now it even made more sense.

A crowd of Africans came out to meet them when they finally arrived back at Djoko Punda on Sunday, October 15. These people looked good to

Oskar and Sarah even if their shirts were torn above the raffia cloth skirts. Once again it was their smiles that made Oskar and Sarah feel so welcome.

Shortly after their arrival they realized that change and tension were once again in the air. On a Sunday evening Brothers Edgardh and Tollefsen read a request to go to Luebo.

By November first, Oskar and Sarah were also packing and preparing for a return stay at Luebo and from there to visit friends and relatives in Sweden and the United States if wartime travel permitted. It was Sarah's turn for a furlough. However, they had decided they would come back to Congo, the Lord willing, at one place or another! They needed time to rest, think and pray for what might be ahead.

As Oskar packed boxes into the storeroom he was amazed at all the belongings he and Sarah now shared.

"You can tell I'm not a bachelor anymore," he chuckled as he counted the baggage and crates they would take with them. It came to about 40 pieces.

Some things they were sending to Kalamba.

The evening before their departure Oskar and Sarah were invited to have supper with the Haighs.

During the supper of simple foods, grown and hunted in the area with the help of shipped in staples, they recalled happy and sad moments they had shared together.

"Remember the Christmas when little Lawrence was so ill and you nursed him back to health," Mrs. Haigh commented.

Oskar nodded. He recalled that bleak Christmas. "It was only through the help of God and the prayers of all of you."

Oskar recalled later that Brother Haigh had said, "I am perfectly satisfied with the work you and your wife have done here." It seemed that some of the old hurts and disagreements had vanished.

At 5:30 a.m. on November 4, 1916, Oskar and Sarah trekked down to the boat that would begin their trip. Porters carried trunks, crates and motley satchels. Tears were in Oskar and Sarah's eyes. They looked around at the gardens, the palm trees, the grave of Brother Stevenson and the Jansens' baby. More tears came as they thought of their own baby and noted all the Africans who had come to say farewell.

"Lots of sad and happy memories here during my four years," Sarah said as she watched where she walked. A soft smile came to her face as she remembered Stevenson's shoes. "But finding you here was the best part of it," she added.

"And I think I'm leaving here with the best single woman missionary that the Congo Inland Mission ever sent."

Epilogue

"But how I miss my very beloved Sarah. The roses have
blossom (sic) extraordinarly (sic) on her grave these years."
Letter from Oskar Andersson to author
September 5, 1972

After taking a furlough to visit their homelands and extended families,
Oskar and Sarah returned to the Belgian Congo. This time they worked
under the Svenska Baptist Missionen (Swedish Baptist Mission Board or
Baptist Union of Sweden) from 1918 to 1948.

Oskar and Sarah never had a living child of their own. Sarah had a later
miscarriage or stillbirth, reportedly twins. No one really knows how many
orphans Sarah took under her motherly wing. One niece remembers 18
raised by Sarah. Pictures frequently show her holding a child or two. Britta
was the first child we hear about after the boy mentioned in this book, plus
at least Morris, Susi and Lasse who we see named from time to time in letters and pictures.

Sarah turned her love for children into this raising of orphans and continuing her work in nursing and midwifery.

Together Oskar and Sarah worked in the Congo at Bendela, Boshwe
and Duma among other locations. They often pioneered the work, building temporary houses, schools and continuing medical and evangelistic
work.

According to one source approximately 5000 persons were led to the saving knowledge of Jesus Christ and Christian growth through their work in the Congo, combined with the efforts of others.

Oskar reported in an article in the *Congo Missionary Messenger* that he had helped to make 200,000 bricks during his stay at Djoko Punda. This was together with helpful African workers.

In a letter to Rev. John Neufeld, of Chicago, Oskar stated, "We thank God too for the privilege (Sic) we twice had of revisiting the field of the C.I.M.—the mission of our first love in Congo."[1]

Sarah died in Sweden, June 18, 1969. Oskar died there November 29, 1979. At her funeral one African student said, "We have had only one 'Mama Sarah' in our mission, and we never will have another like her."[2]

They also had '*Mulunda Wetu*', our friend, in Oskar.

ENDNOTES

Chapter 2

1. Sarah Kroeker, *Texas Hurricane of Sept. 8, 1900,* p. 6. No copyright date or publisher given.

Chapter 6

1. *The Wall Street Journal,* Saturday morning edition, April 20, 1912, (New York, NY: dow Jones & Co.) p. 7.
2. John P. Barkman, "Farewell Song" in notebook of Catherine Neufeld.
3. Sarah Andersson, private letter to John and Catherine Neufeld, August 10, 1957.
4. Andersson, Sarah, letter, August 10, 1957.

Chapter 7

1. Congo Inland Mission Board, *Twenty-five Years of Mission Work in the Belgian Congo.* William B. Weaver and Harry E. Bertsche, Edited by C.E. Rediger, (Chicago, Illinois: Congo Inland Mission, 1938) p. 36.

Chapter 8

1. Oskar Andersson, unpublished diary, August 14, 1914 to November 4, 1916. p. 1, August 14, 1914.

Chapter 9

1. Andersson, diary, p. 2, August 23, 1914.

Chapter 15

1. Andersson, diary, p. 15, December 25, 1914.

Chapter 20

1. Mary Wiens Toews, *Glances Into Congoland* (Inman, Kansas: Salem Publishing House, 1953), p. 25.
2. Andersson, diary, p. 28, May 7, 1915.

Chapter 21

1. Andersson, diary, p. 30, May 27, 1915.

Chapter 24

1. Andersson, diary, p. 38, August 14, 1915.

2. Andersson diary, p, 38, August 14, 1915.

Chapter 27

1. Andersson, diary, p. 43, September 18, 1915.

Chapter 29

1. Andersson, diary, p. 47, October 23, 1915.

2. Andersson, diary, p. 49, November 10, 1915.

Chapter 32

1. Andersson, diary, p. 73, June 17, 1916.

Chapter 34

1. Andersson, diary, p. 83, October 13, 1916.

2. Andersson, diary, p. 83, October 11, 1916.

Epilogue

1. Oskar Andersson, private letter to Rev. John Neufeld, January 21, 1961.

2. Oskar Andersson, private letter to the author, September 1972.

READINGS AND SOURCES

Anderson, Rev. Oscar. "A Few Impressions and Reminiscences From Our Time and Work in C.I.M. at Djoko Punda, 1914-1916 Put Down in a Subjective Way." *The Congo Missionary Messenger,* July-August 1953, Vol. XXIII No. 4.

Anderson, Sarah Kroeker, R.N. "Beginnings of Congo Inland Mission As Told By Mrs. Sarah Kroeker Anderson, R.N." *The Congo Missionary Messenger,* July-August 1953, Vol. XXIII No. 4.

Andersson, Oskar. Unpublished diary. August 14, 1914-November 4, 1916. First English translation by Agri Nilsson. African and English corrections by Elvina Neufeld Martens, M.D. Courtesy of Africa Inter-Mennonite Mission.

Bowman, Martha B. *Ebony Madonna*. Elgin, Illinois: The Brethren Press, 1962.

Carpenter, George Wayland. *HIGHWAYS FOR GOD IN CONGO*. Leopoldville, Belgian Congo: LECO Press, 1952.

Congo Inland Mission Board. *Twenty Five Years of Mission Work in the Belgian Congo*. William B. Weaver and Harry E. Bertsche. Edited by C. E. Rediger. Chicago, Illinois: Congo Inland Mission, 1938.

Field Committee Minutes in their Original Form. Jan. 27, 1913-1936. Africa Inter-Mennonite Mission Collection. Bluffton College Archives, Bluffton, Ohio.

Gerhart, Bob. "Seventy Five Years of Partnership." News Service release from Africa Inter-Mennonite Mission, Elkhart, Indiana: 1986.

HOW IT ALL BEGAN. Play from Congo Inland Mission (Africa Inter-Mennonite Mission). No copyright, date, author or publisher given.

Keidel, Levi O. *WAR TO BE ONE*. Grand Rapids, Michigan: Zondervan Corporation, 1977.

Kroeker Family Book. No editor listed. 1970.

Kroeker, Sarah. *Texas Hurricane of Sept. 8, 1900*. Printed booklet. No copyright, date or publisher given.

Loewen, Melvin J. The Congo Inland Mission 1911-1961. (A dissertation in Partial Fulfillment of the Requirements for the Degree Docteur en Sciences Politiques Presented to La Faculte des Sciences Sociales Politiques et Economiques de L. Universite Libre de Bruxelles) June, 1961. Africa Inter-Mennonite Mission Collection. Bluffton College Archives, Bluffton, Ohio.

Loewen, Melvin J. *THREE SCORE* The Story of an Emerging Mennonite Church in Central Africa. Elkhart, Indiana: Congo Inland Mission. Bethel Publishing Company, 1972.

Neufeld, Catherine. Looseleaf notebook of hymns and clippings.

Neufeld, Elmer. *The Unfinished Revolution,* Congo History and Missionary-African Relations Today. REPORT. Spring, 1963 Vol. VI, No. 1. Akron, Pennsylvania: Mennonite Central Committee.

Records of the Congo Inland Mission Board Organized March 22, 1914. Africa Inter-Mennonite Mission Collection, Bluffton College Archives. Bluffton, Ohio.

Schlabach, Joetta Handrich. *Extending the Table...* A World Community Cookbook. Scottdale, PA: Herald Press, 1991.

Shaw, Trevor R. *CONGO* The thrilling story of 80 years of bringing hope and life to Central Africa. Published by the Protestant Council, Leopoldville, Belgian Congo: Printed by L' Avenir, 1958.

Toews, Mary Wiens. *Glances Into Congoland*. Inman, Kansas: Salem Publishing House, 1953.

Toews, Mary Wiens. *Light Comes to the Congo*. Junior Mission Lessons. Editor Joanna S. Andres. (Prepared under the auspices of the Committee on Education in Church, Home and Community. Board of Education and Publication, General Conference Mennonite Church, 1954.)

Voth, Norma Jost. *MENNONITE FOODS & FOLKWAYS FROM SOUTH RUSSIA* Volumes I and II. Intercourse, PA: Good Books, 1991.
The Wall Street Journal. Saturday morning edition, April 20, 1912. P. 7 "Titanic Dead Total 1635." New York, NY: dow Jones & Co.

Oskar's home and family, Oskar is in front of the ladder.

1. Oskar's home area. Schoolhouse where Oskar attended for six years. From author's files.

2. Sarah as a young woman. From Mary Wiens Toews.

3. Sarah in London with triplets mentioned in book. From author's files.

Mittagsrast auf einer Evangelisationsreise

Cannot understand why the agent does not send bills. They must be here any day now.

Brieg
Bez. Breslau
Feldstrasse 10

mr stevenson

God is scarce now as the station that they depend largely on monkey meat. We will also clear to Antwerp. Am very busy and must stamper. I sleep time. God is good. Will send my picture cala springs and

4. Card showing early work at Djoko Punda station. From author's files.

5. Wedding picture of Oskar and Sarah. From author's files.

6. Travel in the Congo. From Aganetha F. Kroeker.

7. Early brickyard in the Congo. From author's files.

8. Village of Djoko Punda Mission station on hill. From author's files.

9. Oskar and Sarah with some orphans they raised. From author's files.

10. Sarah's 80th birthday in Sweden. From author's files.

11. Grave of Oskar and Sarah in Sweden. Photo sent by Rev. and Mrs. Tare Karlsson.

Picture Credits

1. Oskar' s home area. Schoolhouse where Oskar attended for six years. From author's files.
2. Sarah as a young woman. From Mary Wiens Toews.
3. Sarah in London with triplets mentioned in book. From author's files.
4. Card showing early work at Djoko Punda station. From author's files.
5. Wedding picture of Oskar and Sarah. From author's files.
6. Travel in the Congo. from Aganetha F. Kroeker.
7. Early brickyard in the Congo. From author's files.
8. Village of Djoko Punda. Mission station on hill. From author's files.
9. Oskar and Sarah with some of the orphans they raised. From author's files.
10. Sarah's 80th birthday in Sweden. From author's files.
11. Grave of Oskar and Sarah in Sweden. Photo sent by Rev, and Mrs. Tare Karlsson.

Thanks to all those who over the years sent pictures for which I do not have credits.

Picture following readings and sources is from Oskar.